# Windows 10 Plain & Simple

SECOND EDITION

*Nancy Muir Boysen*
*Michael Miller*

**Windows 10 Plain & Simple**
Published with the authorization of Microsoft Corporation by:
Pearson Education, Inc.

ISBN-13: 978-1-5093-0673-2
ISBN-10:     1-5093-0673-0
Library of Congress Control Number: The LOC is on file.
1 18

**Trademarks**
Microsoft and the trademarks listed at http://www.microsoft.com on the "Trademarks" webpage are trademarks of the Microsoft group of companies. All other marks are property of their respective owners.

**Warning and Disclaimer**

**Special Sales**
For information about buying this title in bulk quantities, or for special sales opportunities (which may include electronic versions; custom cover designs; and content particular to your business, training goals, marketing focus, or branding interests), please contact our corporate sales department at corpsales@pearsoned.com or (800) 382-3419.
For government sales inquiries, please contact governmentsales@pearsoned.com.
For questions about sales outside the U.S., please contact intlcs@pearson.com.

**Editor-in-Chief:** Greg Wiegand
**Acquisitions Editor:** Laura Norman
**Development Editor:** Rick Kughen
**Managing Editor:** Sandra Schroeder
**Senior Project Editor:** Tracey Croom
**Copy Editor:** Wordsmithery

**Indexer:** Valerie Haynes Perry
**Proofreader:** Dan Foster
**Technical Editor:** Laura Acklen
**Editorial Assistant:** Cindy Teeters
**Cover Designer:** Twist Creative, Seattle
**Compositor:** Danielle Foster

# Contents

**5**

**6**

## 24    Troubleshooting ................................................... 271

# Acknowledgments

**From Nancy Boysen, 1st edition:** I'd like to thank Rosemary Caperton at Microsoft Press for trusting me with the writing of this book. Also, much gratitude to Carol Dillingham, who managed the editorial aspects of the book with great grace and professionalism. Many thanks to the folks at Octal Publishing who handled with great competence all the day-to-day production work on this challenging visual book. Thanks to Ed Bott for providing assistance with select figures. Finally, thanks to my technical reviewer, Randall Galloway, for keeping me on track with Windows 10.

**From Michael Miller:** I'd like to thank the entire team at Microsoft Press for helping to turn this manuscript into a printed book. In particular, thanks to Laura Norman, Rick Kughen, and technical editor Laura Acklen, old friends all— a team who really knows how to put a good book togeether.

# About the authors

Nancy Muir Boysen is the author of more than 100 books on technology and other nonfiction topics. Prior to her authoring career, Nancy was a senior manager at several technology publishers as well as a training manager at Symantec. She has a Certificate in Distance Learning Design from the University of Washington, and has taught Internet safety and technical writing at the university level.

Michael Miller is a popular and prolific writer. He has written more than 200 books over the past three decades, on a variety of topics from computers to music to business, for audiences ranging from high school seniors to seniors over 50. He is known for his casual, easy-to-read writing style and his ability to explain a wide variety of complex topics to an everyday audience. Collectively, his books have sold more than a million copies worldwide.

His best-selling technology-related books include *Computer Basics: Absolute Beginner's Guide*, *Easy Computer Basics*, *How Microsoft Windows Vista Works*, *Microsoft Windows XP for Home Users*, *My Smart Home for Seniors*, *My Social Media for Seniors*, *My Windows 10 Computer for Seniors*, *Using Microsoft Windows 95*, and *Windows 7 Your Way*. Learn more about Michael Miller and his books at www.millerwriter.com. His Twitter handle is @molehillgroup.

# About this book

# 1

With Windows 10, Microsoft has created a brand-new computing experience, the culmination of all the Windows products throughout the years. Before Windows 10, you might have used any number of earlier versions, such as Windows 8.1, Windows 8, Windows 7, or Windows Vista. This book is designed to help you make the leap and understand how to find what you need and get things done. Knowing the ins and outs of working with Windows 10 will help you be more efficient when working with your computer.

In this book, you'll find a visual learning experience that offers step-by-step instructions along with images of Windows screens and callouts for each step. You'll always know where to take an action because you can see just what to click or select in apps, the Windows 10 desktop, the Start menu, and so on.

If you're new to Windows, this book will get you going. If you have used previous versions of Windows, you're going to appreciate this very powerful operating system that offers a wealth of functionality and, in many cases, fun and connections with others.

## In this section:

- A quick overview
- A few assumptions
- What's new in Windows 10?
- The final word

# A quick overview

*Windows 10 Plain & Simple* is organized into multiple sections. Each section concerns a specific facet of Windows, and each has a color-coded bar across the top of the page; those colors match the section name in the table of contents. To help you find your way around the contents, here's a quick overview of what each section covers.

Section 2, "First look at Windows 10," introduces the various visual interfaces of Windows 10, such as the Desktop, Start menu, Task View, and Action Center. You also learn how to start Windows 10, log in to your account, and shut down Windows.

Section 3, "Navigating Windows 10," helps you get started using Windows 10. You'll learn how to create new user accounts if your computer is used by people other than you, how to add passwords, and how to open the Windows Settings app, where you can control a variety of features. You are also introduced to Cortana, the personal assistant and search feature new to Windows 10. You get a closer look at the elements on the Start menu, which you use to access apps and settings. Along the way, you get advice about using the taskbar, Task View, setting the date and time, and managing power and storage options.

Section 4, "Customizing the appearance of Windows 10," is where you discover how you can make Windows look the way you prefer. In this section, you adjust desktop themes, colors, background, and text. You also learn how to change screen resolution and customize the taskbar, as well as work with tiles in the Start menu.

Section 5, "Working with productivity applications," explores working with applications such as Microsoft Word, Excel, and PowerPoint. You discover how to open, close, and uninstall apps, as well as how to work with app features such as menus and toolbars. In this section, you also learn about saving, sharing, and printing files.

Section 6, "Finding content with File Explorer and Cortana," is all about finding what you need, both on your computer and online. You find your way around File Explorer, the Windows app that helps you move through the hierarchy of files and folders on your computer and storage drives. You use Cortana to search your computer for files, apps, or settings, and search the web for just about anything.

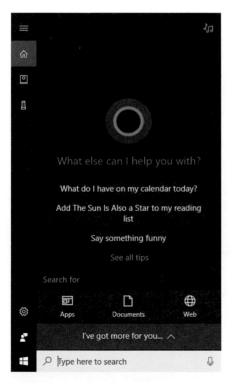

Section 7, "Making Windows accessible," is all about features that make it easier to work on a computer if you have vision, hearing, or dexterity challenges. Here, you learn about adjusting screen contrast and brightness, modifying mouse and keyboard settings to make them easier to handle, using Speech Recognition, Narrator, and more.

Section 8, "Accessing and managing networks," shows you how to get up to speed with networking basics. You learn how to set up your own network and connect to a public network. You discover how to make settings to keep your network secure, and learn how to turn Airplane Mode on and off so that your laptop won't try to connect to a network while you're on a plane.

Section 9, "Going online with Microsoft Edge," introduces you to Microsoft's new web browser. You learn to navigate among websites, use Reading View, and manage multiple tabs. Browsing raises security concerns, so you also learn about blocking pop-up windows, clearing your browsing history, and configuring other security settings. Finally, you learn how to use Web Note, a new feature to mark-up webpages and share them.

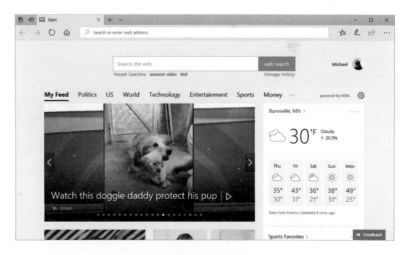

Section 10, "Connecting with others," focuses on Windows' useful People app. This provides a contact database that lets you add and retrieve information about people and organizations with which you interact.

Section 11, "Using Mail," explores the Mail app built in to Windows 10. After you set up your email accounts in Mail, you can read messages from multiple email accounts; create, format, and send new messages; and organize email messages into folders.

Section 12, "Shopping for apps in the Microsoft Store," shows you how to use the online Microsoft Store to read reviews from other users and try out apps before you buy. After you have found an app that you want to buy, this section shows you how to buy and rate that app.

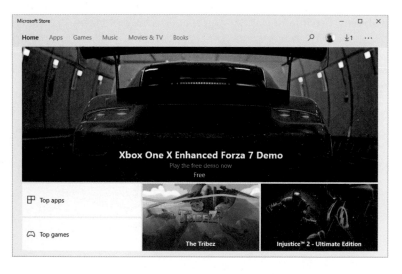

Section 13, "Enjoying music," introduces you to the Groove Music app, which enables you to play your own music and create playlists of your favorite tunes. This section also covers adjusting the volume of your device for the best listening experience.

Section 14, "Recording and watching videos," involves working with the video setting of the Camera app in conjunction with your computer's built-in camera. You also explore how to play movies and other videos via the Movies & TV app.

Section 15, "Working with the Camera and Photos apps," shows you how to take photos and then organize and edit them. You also explore sharing photos with others, creating Story Remixes from your photos, and using a photo as your Lock screen background.

Section 16, "Keeping on schedule with Calendar," helps you explore various Calendar views, create and edit an event, and display the Holidays and Birthdays calendars. You also learn how to create a new event using Cortana, the Windows 10 personal assistant.

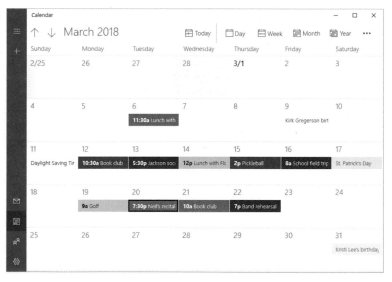

Section 17, "Tracking your sports, news, and stocks," looks at several popular apps built in to Windows 10. You find out about adding favorite sports teams or news sources, using financial tools to track your investments and view stock market activity, and read articles about your interests.

Section 18, "Checking the weather," examines all the features of the Windows 10 Weather app, including turning on Location and Location History, and searching for directions. You discover how to change map styles, zoom in and out, and place a pin on a map.

Section 19, "Using Maps," explores the Maps app, which helps you get where you want to go in the world by providing directions for driving, walking, and even taking public transit. If you grant Maps permission to pinpoint your location, it can more accurately provide directions to and from your location. You can even view 3D maps of certain cities around the world.

Section 20, "Playing with Xbox games," is where you can explore the world of gaming in Windows 10. Using the Xbox app, you can buy games, add friends, and create your own gaming name and avatar. After you begin playing, you can track your achievements and send messages to your friends.

Section 21, "Adding and working with other devices," shows you how to add devices such as printers and scanners. You learn the ins and outs of connecting with Bluetooth devices (which can operate only at short range) and removing devices. Finally, you are introduced to Device Manager and find out how to change device properties and download the latest device drivers.

Section 22, "Working with OneDrive," covers the basics of using the Microsoft OneDrive online file-sharing app. You learn to create folders, upload files, search for files, share files or folders, and rename or delete content from OneDrive.

Section 23, "Maintaining and protecting your computer," looks at several procedures that are important for ensuring that you keep your data and computer protected and its systems maintained. You learn how to get manual updates for Windows 10 between automatic updates, and use tools to clear out unused files or organize data on your hard disk for better performance. You also learn about security features, including Windows Defender and Windows Firewall.

Section 24, "Troubleshooting," addresses situations in which your computer is experiencing problems. In that case, you can use tools to reset and restore your computer or get remote assistance. You can look for help or modify startup options to reboot your computer from a USB stick or DVD drive. In the worst case, you might choose to reinstall Windows and start again.

## A few assumptions

To provide the information you need but not bore you with information you already have, I've made a few assumptions. For example, I assume that you have worked with a computer before and that you know how to use a mouse and keyboard. I don't assume that you have used a touchscreen computer, so although I provide guidance in Section 3 on touchscreen gestures that you can use in Windows 10, most steps are described based on a mouse and keyboard combination.

I also assume that you have worked with some kind of software before, using drop-down menus, toolbars, and dialog boxes to get things done. To use this book and get the most out of Windows 10, you should have an Internet connection and have explored the Internet in the past.

I expect that you are a visual learner who wants information provided in a straightforward, easy-to-understand style as well as tips to make you a better Windows user. No matter how technical you are, I assume that you want to get up to speed on Windows 10 quickly, and without serious effort.

## What's new in Windows 10?

If you're coming from Windows 8.1 or Windows 8, some of Windows 10 will be familiar to you, such as tiles for accessing apps and improved support for touchscreens. If you're migrating from an earlier version of Windows, you'll be glad to see the familiar Start menu, albeit sporting a more graphical look.

What's new to users of all previous versions of Windows is the way that settings that used to be in the Control Panel now reside in the Settings app. Also, Task View displays all open apps, helping you to multitask easily. Within Task View, you can create multiple desktops so that you can return to any one of them and have just the apps you want at the moment, already open on that desktop.

The Action Center contains notifications as well as some short-cuts to common settings such as connecting to a network, brightening the screen, or turning Location services or Airplane Mode on or off.

Perhaps the biggest news in Windows 10 is Cortana, a personal assistant and search feature that learns about your activities and preferences and provides information, search results, and even jokes on request. You can interact with Cortana verbally, or by typing a word or phrase in her Search box. You can also ask Cortana to open apps, play music, send an email, make an appointment, and much, much more.

And if you've been using Windows 10 for a while, you'll be pleased to note several new features and improvements in the Fall Creators Update, released in October 2017. These include new Story Remixes in the Photos app, improvements to Cortana and Microsoft Edge, the capability to send and receive SMS texts via your computer, and being able to add your favorite contacts to the Windows taskbar. We'll cover all these—and more—in this book.

# The final word

Computers and the Internet open a world of opportunity and
entertainment. With Windows 10 and its many apps, you have
an operating system that integrates functionality, creativity, and
sharing in a brand-new way. Whether you use your computer to
listen to music, go online, write reports, or keep up with news
and sports, Windows 10 will make your experience better.

In this book, I've tried to provide a plain and simple visual learning tool that will help you master Windows 10 quickly and easily.
I hope that you profit from this book and find that its design and
organization enhance your learning and enjoyment.

# First look at Windows 10

# 2

Windows 10 represents a leap for Microsoft, but not just from version number 8.1 to 10 (skipping 9 entirely). In fact, Windows 10 is a combination of users' favorite features for the operating system that creates the most seamless way for you to interact with your computer that Microsoft has ever provided. (And the latest version of Windows 10, the Fall Creators Update, adds even more useful features and functionality.)

With Windows 10, you find the traditional Windows desktop and Start menu integrated with features such as Task View (which you use to look at and switch among all open apps), the Action Center (for accessing various settings and notifications), and multiple desktops so that you can construct different "ecosystems" of programs and apps for each use. Windows 10 emphasizes using integrated touchscreen devices such as smartphones, tablets, and touchscreen-enabled computers to make computing a very natural experience, but you can still perform any activity without a touchscreen computer by using a mouse and keyboard.

## In this section:

- Starting Windows 10 for the first time
- Signing in to your user account
- Signing in with a different user account
- Understanding the desktop
- Getting an overview of Tablet Mode and Continuum
- Using the Start menu
- Working with Task View
- Using multiple desktops
- Opening the Action Center
- Working with settings in the Action Center
- Shutting down Windows 10

## Starting Windows 10 for the first time

The first time you press the power button to turn on a computer with Windows 10 installed, you're prompted (both onscreen and via the Cortana voice-activated assistant) to provide some basic information in order to proceed. Follow the onscreen or voice instructions to set your region, keyboard layout, and so forth. Your computer then goes online to check for any updates and downloads and installs them if necessary. You're then asked how you'd like to set up your computer—for personal use or for an organization. Make your choice, then continue to create or sign in to an existing Microsoft account, set up a PIN, choose privacy settings, and so forth.

Follow the instructions and make the appropriate choices, and you'll have everything configured in a matter of minutes. You'll then be logged in to Windows and presented with the Windows desktop, ready for use.

How would you like to set up?

Set up for personal use
We'll help you set it up with a personal Microsoft account. You'll have full control over this device.

Set up for an organization
You'll gain access to your organization's resources like email, network, apps, and services. Your organization will have full control over this device.

**TIP** You can modify any of the settings that Windows 10 implements, such as date, time, or language after you begin using Windows. To modify the date, time, or language settings, for example, click the Start button, click Settings, and then click Time & Language.

## Signing in to your user account

Your user account is set up when you first start Windows 10. You can create additional user accounts for Windows so that different people who use your computer can save their unique files and Windows settings. When you turn off your computer or it goes to sleep after a period of inactivity, you are signed out of the currently active user account and presented with a Lock screen. You need to type a password to sign in to Windows as the last active user or as another user. If you set up a PIN (a 4-digit code alternative to a password) in Settings, you can provide that instead of a password.

### Sign in

**1**  Click anywhere on the Lock screen.

**2**  Type the password or PIN and then press Enter.

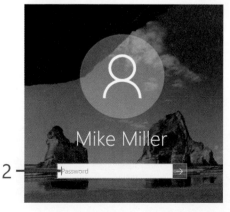

# Signing in with a different user account

When you have created more than one user (see Section 3, "Navigating Windows 10," for more about this), you can sign in as another user to open Windows with that person's unique settings and files. You do this from the same Windows sign-in screen shown in the previous task.

## Sign in as a different user

**1** Click the Lock screen to display the sign-in screen.

**2** Click the user name of the account to which you want to sign in.

**3** Type a password to sign in as that user.

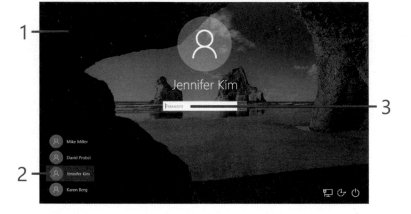

**TIP** To create other user accounts, click the Start button, click Settings, and then click Accounts. You can create as many accounts as you like, each one preserving settings and documents unique to that account. You can also set up a password or PIN for signing in. See "Setting up accounts" on page 24 for details about this process.

## Understanding the desktop

Whereas Windows 7 had a single desktop and Start menu, and Windows 8 had a desktop and a Start screen but no Start menu, Windows 10 strikes a happy medium; this version of Windows has a single desktop with a Start menu that you can expand to a full screen. If you're working primarily on the desktop, you can access common commands and apps through the redesigned Start menu.

The desktop in Windows 10 also retains the traditional taskbar along the bottom, desktop shortcuts for items such as the Recycle Bin, and a few added features, such as Cortana, the new personal assistant that can help you accomplish many tasks. When turned on, Cortana appears on the left side of the taskbar and looks like a search box in which you can enter a search term and get results related to files on your computer or content on the web. But Cortana offers much more. You can wake Cortana by saying, "Hey, Cortana," or by clicking the microphone button on the right side of the Cortana search box. You can also type a question or term in the box and Cortana will find matching results. If you turn off the Cortana feature, the box acts as a straightforward search tool.

To the right of the Cortana search box is the Task View button. Click this button to view thumbnails of all open apps on the desktop, helping you to switch among them quickly. Finally, the new Action Center button, located on the right side of the taskbar, opens the Action Center, which is a slide-out panel that lists notifications about items such as new email or upcoming appointments. It also offers an expandable set of buttons that provide access to Windows settings.

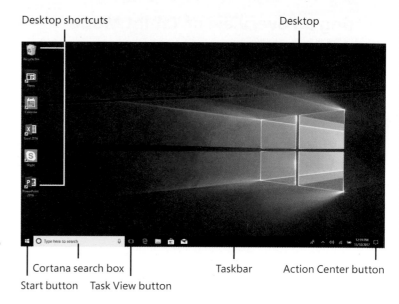

Desktop shortcuts          Desktop

Cortana search box          Taskbar          Action Center button

Start button     Task View button

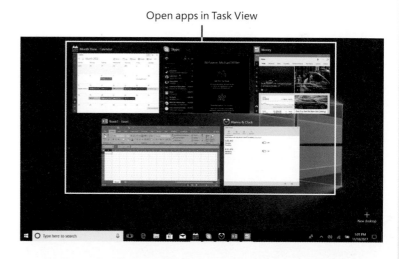

Open apps in Task View

# Getting an overview of Tablet Mode and Continuum

One of the settings you access through the Action Center is Tablet Mode, which makes it possible to work with a touch-screen interface without having to use a physical keyboard or mouse. Tablet Mode displays open apps in a full-screen view rather than in individual windows. Also, when Tablet Mode is active and you click the Start button, the expanded Start menu is displayed.

You can display Tablet Mode on any computer, not just a tablet. When you work with a Windows tablet such as Micro-soft Surface or if you have a 2-in-1 laptop that converts to a tablet configuration, this mode is very handy.

When you remove or switch from the keyboard functionality of a tablet or laptop, the Continuum feature kicks in automati-cally, displaying all open apps in Tablet Mode.

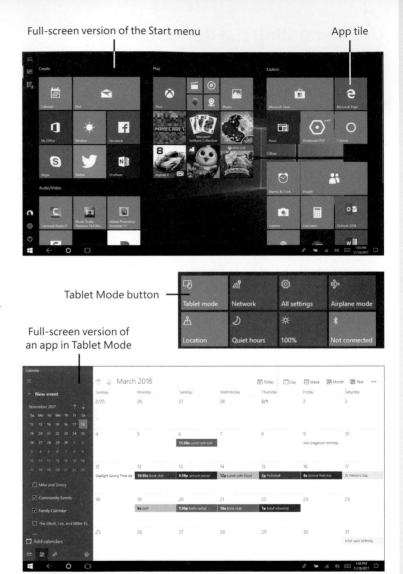

Full-screen version of the Start menu

App tile

Tablet Mode button

Full-screen version of an app in Tablet Mode

## Using the Start menu

The Start menu provides access to all the apps installed on your computer. Also, the Start menu offers a Power button that you can use to put your computer to sleep, restart it, or turn it off altogether. The Start menu also contains tiles that will be familiar to users of the Windows 8 and Windows 8.1 Start Screen; you can click these to access apps such as News, Camera, Groove Music, Mail, and Calendar. (Note that if you are in Tablet Mode— described in the previous task—the Start menu opens to a full-screen view by default; the following steps assume that Tablet Mode is off.)

### Display the Start menu

1  Click the Start button.

2  In the list on the left, click an app from the Recently Used, Most Used, or alphabetical list.

3  Click the Start button again.

4  Click an app tile.

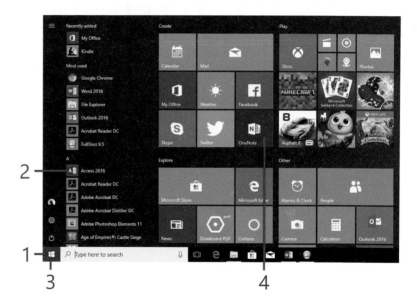

> ✓ **TIP**  You can add labels (which you can later edit) to the sets of tiles to help you identify their content. Click above a set of tiles and then, in the text box that appears, type a label, such as "Online Content" or "Lifestyle Apps." Click anywhere outside of the text box to accept the new label.

# Working with Task View

With Task View, you can view thumbnails of all open apps and switch among them with ease. If, for example, you are using Microsoft Word and you want to make a call on Skype, which you had opened earlier, you can go to Task View without closing Word and jump to the Skype app to make your call. When your call is over, you can use Task View to jump back to the still-open Word app quickly.

## Open Task View and switch between open apps

1   On the taskbar, click the Task View button.

2   Click an app to make it the active app.

---

TIP   An alternative to using the Task View button is to press Alt+Tab on your keyboard. A box appears containing thumbnails of all open apps. While continuing to hold down the Alt key, press Tab to scroll among the open apps. Release both keys to switch to the currently selected app.

# Using multiple desktops

New in Windows 10 is the ability to create and save multiple desktops. For example, you might like to have one set of apps that you use for your hobby and another for your work, but you want to keep those sets of open apps separate. You can create one desktop that displays open apps related to your hobby, another related to the apps you use for work, and so on. You then can easily switch among them.

## Create and display a desktop

1  On the taskbar, click the Task View button.

2  Click New Desktop.

3  Open any apps that you want to appear on this desktop by opening the Start menu and clicking the apps you want to open.

4  To cycle among the desktops, click the Task View button.

5  Click the thumbnail for the desktop you want to open.

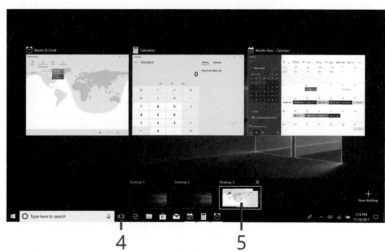

> **TRY THIS**   Use the method described here to create a desktop for work-related apps, another for your family's activities, and another for a hobby such as genealogy or stamp collecting. Show your family or friends how to switch among these desktops.

> **TIP**   To delete a desktop click the Task View button, and then, in the top-right corner of any desktop displayed, click the Close button.

# Opening the Action Center

The Action Center is a useful panel that's new with Windows 10. When you display the Action Center, you see notifications about items, such as new email or upcoming appointments. The Action Center also displays a set of buttons with which you can access all Windows settings or switch on or off several commonly used settings, including Tablet Mode, Airplane Mode, and Bluetooth device connections. You can also adjust your computer's Brightness setting.

## Display the Action Center

**1** On the taskbar, click the Action Center button.

**2** Click a notification to see more details.

**3** Click a setting.

You will see different results depending on which setting you choose:

- Click a setting button to turn it on or off (as with Tablet Mode, Bluetooth, Airplane Mode, Rotation Lock, Wi-Fi, and Location sharing).

- Click a setting button to display a panel for working with those types of settings (as with Network, All Settings, and VPN).

The Brightness setting increases the brightness of your screen with each click. For more control over screen brightness, right-click the Brightness button, and then, in the shortcut menu that appears, click Go To Settings to open a window with display settings, including—on some notebook PCs—a Brightness Level slider.

# Working with settings in the Action Center

If you want to display only the most frequently used settings buttons in the Action Center, you can collapse the set of settings buttons to show less. You then can easily expand this area of the Action Center to display all settings buttons.

## Expand and select settings

1 On the taskbar, click the Action Center button.

2 If there is only one row of settings buttons, click the Expand button to display all settings.

3 Click the Collapse button to show only the top row of settings.

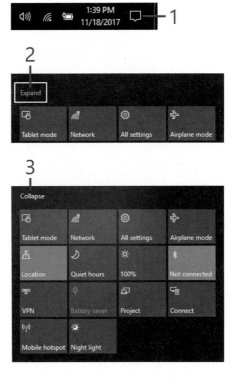

---

✓ **TIP** The All Settings button is your entrée to all Windows settings. See "Accessing Settings" on page 23 to learn more about what this button does.

# Shutting down Windows 10

When you're done working with your computer, you have a few options. You can use the Power button, which is located in the Start menu, to turn off your computer, restart it (which is useful when installing new software or implementing software updates), or put it to sleep. Putting your computer to sleep saves power when you're not using your computer, but lets you get going quickly when you want to use your computer again.

## Work with the Power button

**1** Click the Start button.

**2** Click Power.

**3** Click the option you want: Sleep to temporarily put your computer to sleep; Shut Down to turn off your computer; or Restart to turn off and then turn on your computer (for example, to allow updates to be implemented).

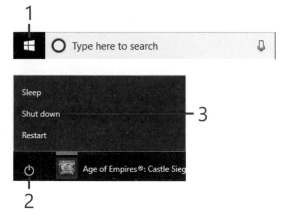

> ✓ **TIP** You can use the Restart option if your computer or an app seems to be experiencing problems. Restarting causes Windows to reboot, which can often solve performance issues. See Section 24, "Troubleshooting," for more about solving computer problems.

# Navigating
# Windows 10

# 3

Beginning to use a new operating system such as Windows 10 is like walking into a new job: You need to figure out where your desk is, where the copier and coffee are, and how to find your coworkers. In Windows, you need to learn how to open and close applications; set up user accounts and passwords so that more than one person can access your computer; provide input with a mouse, keyboard, or touchscreen; and learn how to find and use some of the basic settings and tools available to you.

After you explore the tasks in this section, you'll know the basics of getting around Windows 10, making settings, providing input, and searching for information by using the exciting new personal assistant, Cortana. You also encounter the taskbar, which provides shortcuts to various functions, and the Start menu, which gives you access to all your apps.

## In this section:

- Opening and closing windows
- Accessing Settings
- Setting up accounts
- Managing passwords
- Adding a picture password
- Using a PIN
- Using a touchscreen with Windows 10
- Exploring the Start menu
- Expanding the Start menu
- Exploring the taskbar
- Working with Cortana
- Adjusting system volume
- Managing power options
- Setting the date and time

# Opening and closing windows

There's a good reason why the Windows operating system has its name. When you work with this operating system, you open *windows* to display applications such as Microsoft Word, media players, Internet browsers, files and folders, settings, and more. When you open a window, you can use all the tools and features of that environment. You can also display a window as full screen or in a reduced size (which helps you to work with more than one app at a time), and you can close a window, which closes the application.

## Work with windows

1 Click the Start button.

2 Click the Calendar tile.

3 Click the Maximize button.

4 Click the Minimize button.

5 Click the Close button.

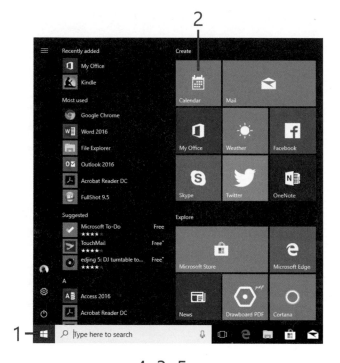

> ✓ **TIP** You can display several reduced windows on your desktop. If you want to view all open apps, on the taskbar, click the Task View button, which then displays all open apps in thumbnails, whether the apps are open full-screen or reduced to a smaller window.

> → **TRY THIS** With a window open, click the Minimize button (it's represented by the dash symbol to the left of the Maximize/Minimize button in the top-right corner of the window). This keeps the app open and available on the taskbar, but the app window does not display on the screen.

# Accessing Settings

In addition to applications, Windows 10 offers its own settings that help you set up new user accounts; open accessibility tools such as Narrator; manage your system, network, and devices; and personalize the look of your desktop and windows. The Settings window is also where you can manage your computer's security and set up the date, time, and language, as well as perform updates to Windows. Consider this like the central command for Windows 10.

## Open and close Settings

**1** Click the Start button.

**2** Click Settings.

**3** Click any category of Settings to display a secondary Settings window for that category.

# Setting up accounts

In many instances, there might be more than one person using a computer, or you might want to use your computer for more than one purpose. When you have multiple users or user cases, you can set up Windows with separate user accounts within which you can save unique settings (such as desktop background), sets of applications, and files. With several user accounts set up, you can, for example, access one account for business and one for personal use, or one for you and one for your spouse/partner. You can even

password-protect accounts so that nobody can open another person's account, thereby preventing your child or brother-in-law from accessing and deleting your valuable investment spreadsheet or much agonized-over novel.

When you first set up Windows 10, a user account is created for you. You can add accounts at any time so long as you're logged-in to an account with administrator privileges.

## Add a new user account

**1** Display Settings.

**2** Click Accounts.

**3** Click Family & Other People.

**4** Scroll to the Other People section and click Add Someone Else to This PC.

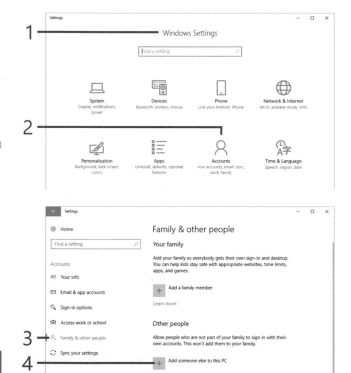

*(continued on next page)*

 **TIP** If you are creating an account for a family member, go to the Your Family section and click—Add a Family Member, instead.

## Add a new user account  *continued*

5  Type an email address that the new person will use to sign in to Windows 10, if you know it.

6  Click Next.

7  Click Finish.

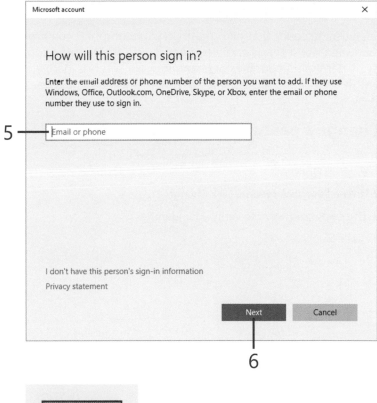

---

TIP   If you are creating a family account for a child and want to use Family Safety settings to get reports on the child's activities on the computer, select the check box labeled Is This a Child's Account? before you click Finish in step 7.

# Managing passwords

Each user account that you create on your computer can have its own separate settings and files. For privacy, and to avoid somebody damaging your files or changing your settings inadvertently, you should protect each user account with a password.

With a password in place, only those who know the password can open a user account. The following steps describe how to change the password; these instructions apply to the account to which you are currently signed in.

## Change a password

1 Go to the Accounts section of Settings, and then click Sign-In Options.

2 In the Password section, click Change.

3 Type your password to verify your identity.

4 Click Sign In.

*(continued on next page)*

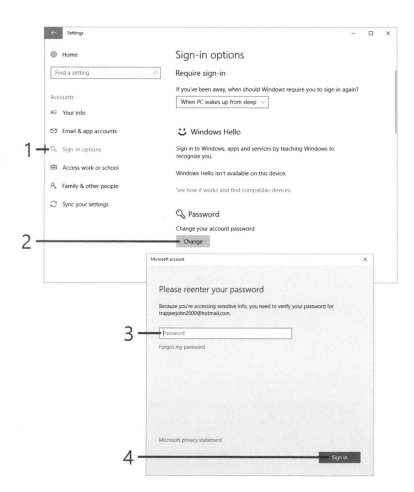

## Change a password *continued*

**5** Type your old password.

**6** Type and confirm your new password.

**7** Click Next.

**8** Click Finish.

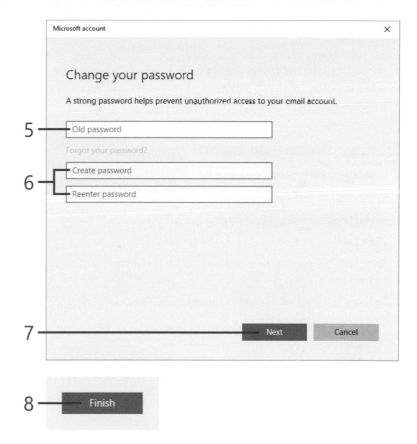

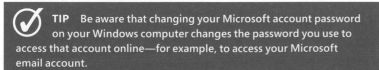

> ✓ **TIP** Be aware that changing your Microsoft account password on your Windows computer changes the password you use to access that account online—for example, to access your Microsoft email account.

# Adding a picture password

If you're more of the visual type and have a touchscreen com-puter, you might prefer to access your account by using a pic-ture rather than by using password characters. With the picture password, you select a picture and then assign three onscreen gestures. For example, if you use a picture of a person, you might draw a smile on the lips and circles around the eyes. The combination of the picture and your gestures thereby becomes your password.

## Create a picture password

**1** In Settings, click Accounts, and then click Sign-In Options.

**2** In the Picture Password section, click Add.

**3** In the Create a Picture Password box, type your current password.

**4** Click OK.

**5** To accept the suggested picture, click Use This Picture and skip to step 10.

**6** To use a different picture, click Choose New Picture.

*(continued on next page)*

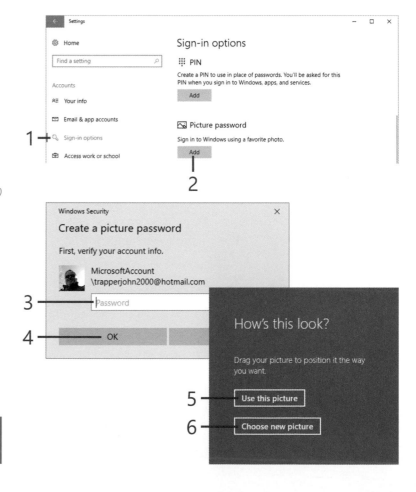

TIP   If you don't have a touchscreen PC, you can use your mouse to draw your picture password.

## Create a picture password  *continued*

**7** Type a name into the File Name box or browse through your files to find a picture to use.

**8** Click Open.

**9** Click Use This Picture.

**10** Using your finger, draw gestures on the touchscreen.

**11** Repeat the gestures to confirm them.

**12** Click Finish.

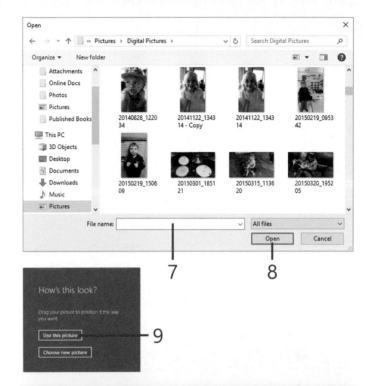

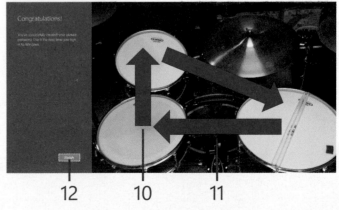

> **TIP** If you decide that you no longer want to use a picture password, in the Accounts window, click the Remove button, located in the Picture Password section.

> **⚠ CAUTION** You must remember your picture password gestures, including the approximate start and end points and the direction to swipe. If you forget your gestures, you won't be able to access your account.

# Using a PIN

Passwords are very useful, but sometimes they contain more characters than you'd care to type each and every time you sign in. If that's the case, you might find a PIN (personal identification number) very useful. A PIN is a four-or-more-digit password, which is typically much shorter and easier to type than a password. A PIN is more secure than a password, too, since it's tied to your specific device.

## Create a PIN

1 Display Settings.

2 Click Accounts.

*(continued on next page)*

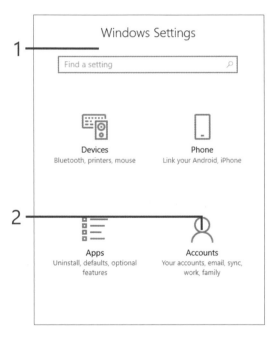

## Create a PIN *continued*

**3** Click Sign-In Options.

**4** In the PIN section, click Add. When prompted, enter your current password.

**5** Type your four digit PIN.

**6** Confirm the PIN.

**7** Click OK.

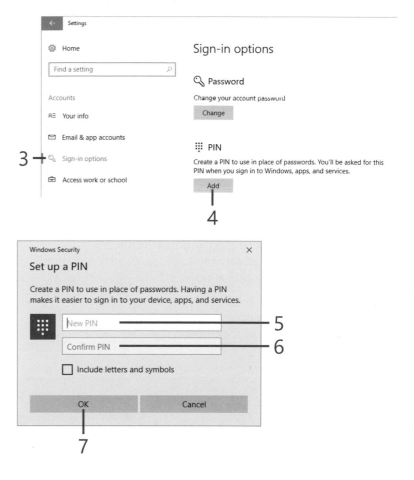

**TIP** You can make a stronger PIN by including letters and symbols in addition to the normal numbers. To do this, enable the Include Letters and Symbols check box.

# Using a touchscreen with Windows 10

If you have a touchscreen computer, you can take advantage of several ways in which Windows 10 is optimized for touch input. Using your finger and touch gestures in place of a mouse or keyboard, you can scroll down a page, make a selection, choose a command or check box, and type using an onscreen keyboard. Using a touchscreen is a natural and efficient way of interacting with your computer.

Here is a list of commonly used touchscreen gestures that you can utilize with your Windows 10 computer:

- Tap to select any item that you'd click with a mouse, such as a check box, drop-down list, on/off slider, or text box. You can also tap to place an insertion point in a document, indicating where the next action is to take place.

- Swipe your finger from the left edge of the screen inward to display Task View.

> ✓ **TIP** In Windows 10, several multi-finger gestures were introduced for use on laptops that have touchpads built in. For example, swiping the touchpad with three fingers displays the Cortana panel, and swiping the touchpad with four fingers opens Action Center.

> ✓ **TIP** Because not everybody has a touchscreen-enabled computer, most of the steps in this book assume the use of a mouse and keyboard, but feel free to substitute a tap whenever a step instructs you to click!

- Swipe your finger from the right edge of the screen inward to display the Action Center.

- Place your fingers together on the screen and spread them apart to enlarge a document or webpage.

- Place your fingers apart on the screen and pinch them together to reduce a document or webpage.

Swipe from left to display Task View

Tap a button to close a window

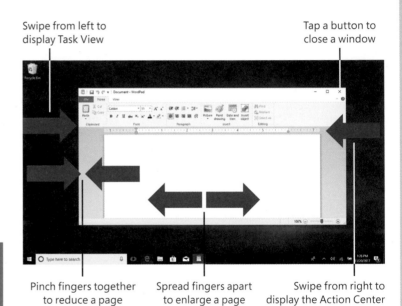

Pinch fingers together to reduce a page

Spread fingers apart to enlarge a page

Swipe from right to display the Action Center

# Exploring the Start menu

The Start menu provides access to all the apps and settings available on your Windows 10 computer. At the bottom of the Start menu, three frequently used items are always available: Settings, Power, and Your Account. All apps are listed alphabetically on the left side of the menu. To the right are sets of tiles that you can click to explore popular apps such as Calendar, News, and Mail.

## Open and make choices from the Start menu

1  Click the Start button.

2  Scroll down the alphabetical list and click an app to open it.

3  Click the Start button again.

4  Click an app tile, such as Weather, to open it.

5  Click the Start button again.

6  Click Power to view a menu of the shutdown and restart options.

7  Click the Settings button to open the Settings window.

TRY THIS  Tiles in the Start menu are organized into groups—for example, Life at a Glance. If you want to rename a group, click the space above a set of tiles. The Title box opens, in which you can type a new name for the tiles in that group.

# Enlarging the Start menu

If you want to see more app tiles without scrolling, you can change the size of the Start menu. You can make the Start menu taller or wider, or both.

## Resize the Start menu

1 Click the Start button.

2 Use your mouse to click and grab the top, right side, or top-right corner of the Start menu.

3 Drag the Start menu to the size you want. The app tiles rearrange themselves automatically.

2, 3

1

# Exploring the taskbar

By default, the taskbar runs across the bottom of the Windows desktop (you can change its location on the screen, which I'll show you how to do in Section 4, "Customizing the appearance of Windows 10"). This small bar contains a wealth of settings, making them available for quick and easy access. It also shows active applications whose windows have been minimized so that you can simply click one to enlarge it. If the taskbar isn't visible, move your mouse pointer to the bottom of the desktop to display it.

The Start button is on the far left of the taskbar. You click this to display the Start menu, from which you can access all the apps installed on your computer. Directly to the right of the Start button is Cortana, the new personal assistant and search feature (covered in the next task).

You use the buttons in the middle of the taskbar to display open apps in Task View, launch pinned apps, or maximize open apps.

Finally, the set of buttons on the right side of the taskbar give you access to settings for features such as power management, network connections, system volume, Action Center, and the Touch Keyboard. You can use the Show Hidden Icons button to display more available settings. Several of these items are covered in more detail later in this section. Action Center is covered in Section 2, "First look at Windows 10," and network settings are covered in Section 8, "Accessing and managing networks."

Start button

Cortana                Task View button                Open apps

System volume

People                Power        Action Center

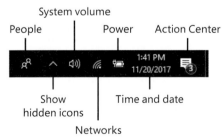

Show
hidden icons              Time and date

Networks

> **✓ TIP**  If you want the taskbar to always remain on the screen, right-click any empty area of the taskbar and then, from the shortcut menu that appears, select Lock the Taskbar. To move the taskbar to another side of the screen, right-click an empty area of the taskbar, click Taskbar Settings, then pull down the Taskbar Location on Screen list and make a selection.

# Working with Cortana

Cortana is a new personal assistant feature in Windows 10 that serves many functions. Using Cortana, you can search for all kinds of items, including files on your computer, online information, and media. Cortana also gives you an overview of your day, which might include appointments, news headlines, local events, and even a suggested restaurant for lunch. In fact, Cortana learns about you as you interact with your computer, so her suggestions become more and more relevant. You can ask Cortana to send an email message, place a call via Skype, or even send a text message to someone's phone.

Cortana provides two means of input: You can type a word, phrase, or question into the Cortana search box, or you can speak to Cortana. Depending on what you type or say, she will either respond verbally or by displaying search results. (Note that the first time you open Cortana, you are asked for permission to let her access your computer and record your name so that she can greet you by name.)

When you ask Cortana for anything, a panel appears with results as well as a set of buttons that you can use to do the following:

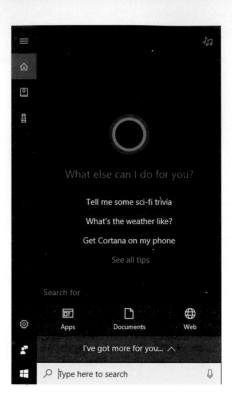

- View a Notebook home page that you can customize to contain items you use often, such as travel information, news headlines, and weather.

- Access saved reminders and create new reminders.

- Ask questions about all sorts of topics.

- Calculate conversions and mathematical problems.

- Find documents on your computer and apps in the Microsoft Store.

**Provide voice and text input for Cortana**

1  Click the Cortana search box.

2  Type a word, phrase, or question.

3  Click the result that you want Cortana to display.

4  On the right side of Cortana's search box, click the microphone.

5  When the Cortana pane appears, speak a word, phrase, or question.

**TRY THIS** Instead of clicking the microphone in the Cortana search box, try saying, "Hey Cortana," followed by a question such as, "When is my next appointment?" As you use Cortana over time, she becomes more accustomed to your voice and the items you access frequently.

# Adjusting system volume

You've probably watched a movie or listened to music on a Windows computer before, so you know that media players have their own volume controls provided within their playback tools. However, your computer also has a system volume control. This control sets the volume of your computer, and thus the volume for individual players is set relative to that master volume (for example, a player volume set at 50 percent is set at 50 percent of the system volume setting). A handy button on the taskbar offers you control over system volume.

## Raise or lower volume

1 On the right side of the taskbar, click the Volume button.

2 Drag the slider to the right to raise the volume.

3 Drag the slider to the left to lower the volume.

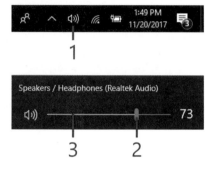

> **TIP** To access separate controls for your speakers and your system sounds (such as alerts for new notifications), right-click the Volume button, and then, in the shortcut menu that opens, select Open Volume Mixer.

# Setting the date and time

Your computer depends on knowing the date and time in your location to do many things. For example, if you have scheduled maintenance tasks such as downloading system updates for a certain time of the day, that time depends on your date and time settings. Your calendar is attuned to the date and time settings, including notifications and alerts. If you travel with your computer or move to a new location, you might want to change the date and time to match your whereabouts.

## Change the date and time

**1**  On the taskbar, right-click the Date and Time section.

**2**  Click Adjust Date/Time.

**3**  Switch off the Set Time Automatically setting.

**4**  Click the Change button under Change Date and Time.

*(continued on next page)*

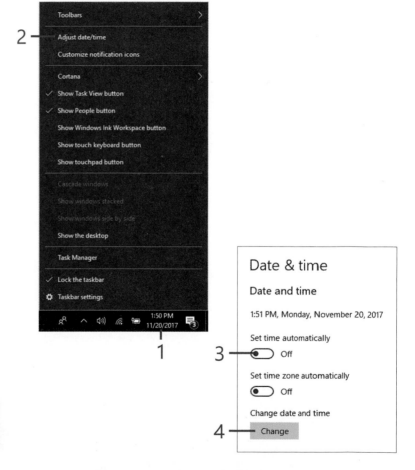

> **TRY THIS**  If you simply want to change your time zone so that the computer adjusts date and time automatically, in step 3, you would instead click Set Time Automatically.

## Change the date and time *continued*

5   Click the drop-down lists to change settings for the Date.

6   Click the drop-down lists to change settings for Time.

7   Click Change to close the Date and Time Settings window.

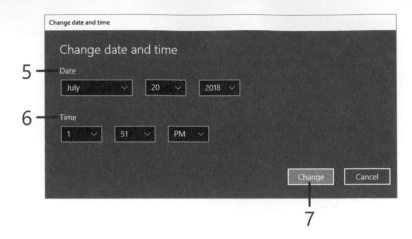

# Managing power options

If you work on a laptop computer or tablet, you need to be aware of the remaining charge in your battery. With Windows 10, you can adjust power options so that your computer conserves energy by adjusting its performance. For example, using a Power Saver plan might maintain your screen brightness at a dimmer setting to help your battery's charge last longer. You can choose which power plan to use, ranging from Power Saver to High

Performance. Power Saver reduces your computer's performance but saves energy. High Performance lets your computer deliver the best performance, but your battery will discharge sooner. You can also adjust the timing of certain actions, such as when Windows puts the computer to sleep, by changing settings for a particular plan.

## Adjust power options

1 On the taskbar, right-click the Power button.

2 Click Power Options.

3 Select the power plan you want to use.

4 Click Change Plan Settings for the selected plan.

(continued on next page)

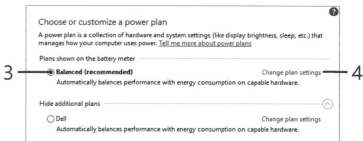

## Adjust power options *continued*

**5** In the On Battery column, select the appropriate drop-down list or slider to choose the timing for turning off the display, putting the computer to sleep, and adjusting plan brightness for when the computer is running on battery.

**6** In the Plugged In column, select the appropriate drop-down list or slider to choose the timing for turning off the display, putting the computer to sleep, and adjusting plan brightness for when the computer is plugged in.

**7** Click Save Changes.

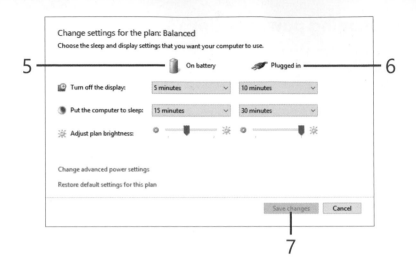

# Customizing the appearance of Windows 10

# 4

Windows 10 is an environment in which you'll spend a lot of time, so being able to set up the appearance of its various elements in ways that please you is a great benefit. You can change the background image for the desktop, colors, the size of text, and more. You can also work with the size and placement of tiles in the Start menu.

Some of these settings customize the desktop appearance, whereas others make working with apps a lot easier. For example, you can arrange open windows on the desktop so that you can view more than one app at a time, which helps when you need to copy and paste contents from one app to another or reference information in one document while working in another. You can customize the taskbar contents such that the icons you need most often are always close at hand. And, of course, you can change the colors and background picture for your desktop.

**In this section:**

- Changing the desktop background
- Customize the Lock screen
- Using themes
- Adjusting colors and transparency
- Changing to the Dark Theme
- Making timeout settings
- Enlarging text
- Changing screen resolution
- Customizing the taskbar
- Adding tiles to the Start menu
- Moving tiles
- Resizing tiles
- Using Snap to arrange apps on the Desktop

# Changing the desktop background

We all like to personalize our work environment, from pinning photos to the wall of a cubicle at work to decorating the walls of our home office. In the same way, Windows 10 provides images that you can use to add visual appeal to your Desktop.

To customize your Windows experience, you can change which Windows images appear as backgrounds, and even use your own images.

## Choose a new background picture

**1** Click the Start button.

**2** Click Settings.

**3** Click Personalization.

*(continued on next page)*

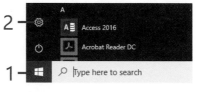

**TIP** To select your own picture as your background in step 6, click the Browse button and then locate a picture of your own using File Explorer. When you've found the picture you want, click the Choose Picture button to select the image.

## Choose a new background picture *continued*

**4** Make sure Background is selected. (It should be, by default.)

**5** Open the Background list and select Picture.

**6** In the Choose Your Picture section, select an existing picture or click Browse to select another picture stored on your computer or OneDrive.

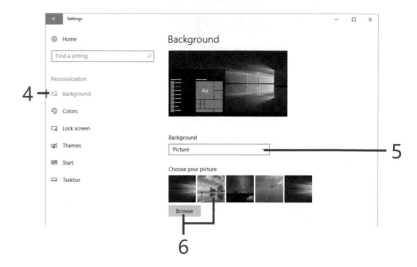

---

✓ **TIP** If you prefer a solid color background to a picture, click the Background drop-down list and choose Solid.

# Customize the Lock screen

The Lock screen appears whenever your computer goes to sleep. When you want to wake up your computer and begin using it again, you see the Lock screen image, which you then click to display a sign-in screen to access Windows 10. You can choose what type of background image appears on the Lock screen: Windows Spotlight, which shows images from the Bing search engine; a Microsoft provided picture; or a slide show of images from your Picture folder or Windows Spotlight.

## Choose a new Lock screen background

**1** In Settings, choose Personalization, and then click Lock Screen.

**2** Click the Background drop-down list and click Picture.

**3** In the Choose Your Picture section, click an image or click Browse to select another image stored on your computer or OneDrive.

---

**✓ TIP** Another option is to let Windows choose your Lock screen pictures for you by selecting Windows Spotlight in step 3. The next time the Lock screen is displayed, in the top-right corner, move your pointer over Like What You See?, and then click either I Like It! or Not a Fan? to cast your vote. The next time you go to Spotlight, you'll see images more like those that you've endorsed. Spotlight can also learn about you and the services and features you use in Windows 10 to make suggestions on the Lock screen about other features or apps that you might enjoy.

# Adjusting colors and transparency

The colors that appear on various elements of your screen (for example, the taskbar and open window borders) have two functions. First, they can appeal to your personal color sense and make your computing environment more attractive. Second, they help make the content on the screen easier to see. You can configure Windows 10 to pick a color scheme that matches the background image you've chosen, select your own custom colors, or make the Start menu transparent. You can also choose from among several high-contrast color schemes that are especially helpful for those who have poor vision.

## Control colors and transparency

1  In Settings, choose Personalization, and then click Colors.

2  To select a specific color for selected screen elements, click a color from the Windows Colors palette.

3  To let Windows choose an appropriate color, enable the Automatically Pick an Accent Color from the My Background check box.

4  If you want the taskbar and other elements to change color (rather than remaining black), scroll down to the Show Accent Color on the Following Surfaces and check the Start, Taskbar, and Action Center and/or Title Bars options.

5  Click to turn on or off the Transparency Effects option.

6  Click High Contrast Settings to choose a color scheme in the Ease of Access settings.

(continued on next page)

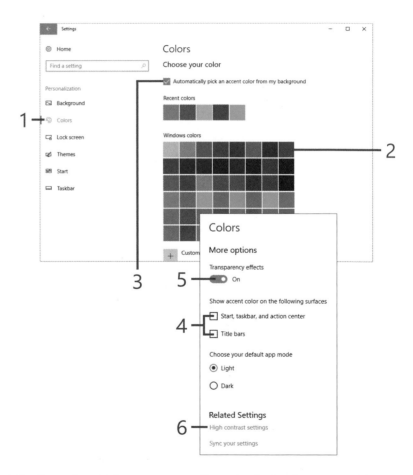

## Control colors and transparency *continued*

**7** In the High Contrast section, click the Choose a Theme list to display available themes.

**8** Click a theme.

**9** To customize your own theme, click any screen element, then

**10** From the palette that opens, choose a color.

**11** Click Done.

**12** Click Apply.

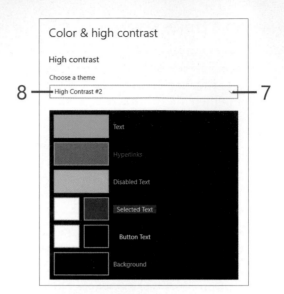

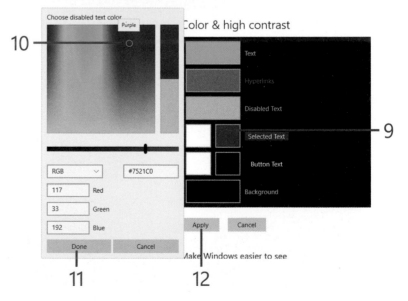

## Changing to Dark Mode

By default, Windows 10 displays most system windows and dialog boxes in Light mode, with black or darker colored text against a white background. Many users prefer the new Dark mode, which reverses that scheme, with white or lighter colored text against a black background.

### Enable Dark Mode

**1** In Settings, choose Personalization, and then click Colors.

**2** In the Choose Your Default App Mode section, click to select Dark.

**3** To return to Light mode, click to select Light.

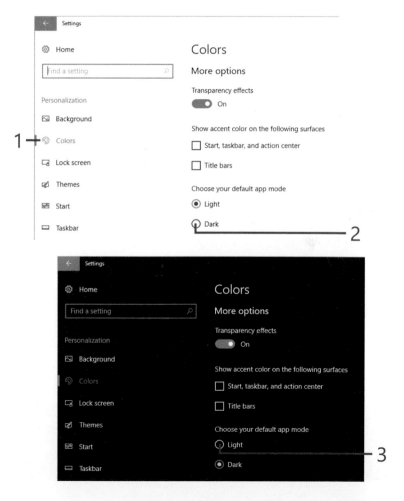

# Using themes

Windows 10 includes several themes that control the appearance of your screen. These themes provide an easy way to apply a variety of settings such as colors, font, and background images to the computer interface.

## Select a theme

**1**  In Settings, choose Personalization, and then click Themes.

**2**  In the Apply a Theme section, click to select an available theme.

**3**  To discover additional themes in the Microsoft Store, scroll to the Get More Personality in Windows section and click Get more Themes.

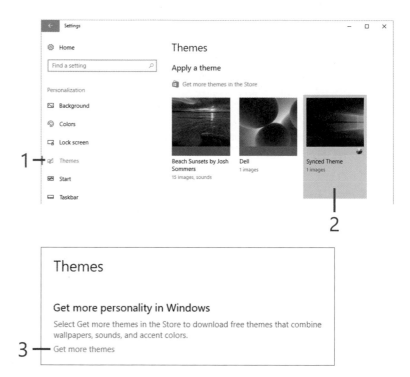

# Adjusting timeout settings

After a certain interval of inactivity, Windows will go to sleep. When your computer is asleep, you must click the Lock screen and then type a password or PIN on the subsequent sign-in screen to access your computer. You might find it disruptive if this happens after a very short interval. Conversely, if Windows waits a long time before it goes to sleep, you might end up draining your laptop battery of power unnecessarily.

You can control how quickly your computer goes to sleep or turns off when it's running on battery power or plugged into a power outlet. Another way in which you can conserve power is by turning your screen off while still leaving the computer on. Although this doesn't save as much energy as when the computer goes to sleep, one benefit of turning off the screen is that it doesn't stop existing apps (such as the Groove Music app) from working, whereas putting your computer to sleep stops apps from running and requires you to sign in again.

## Choose when your screen times out

1 In Settings, choose Personalization, and then click Lock Screen.

2 Scroll down and click Screen Timeout Settings.

3 Click a drop-down list to choose a time interval for when the screen turns off while running on battery or when plugged in.

4 Click a drop-down list to choose a time interval for when the computer goes to sleep while running on battery or when plugged in.

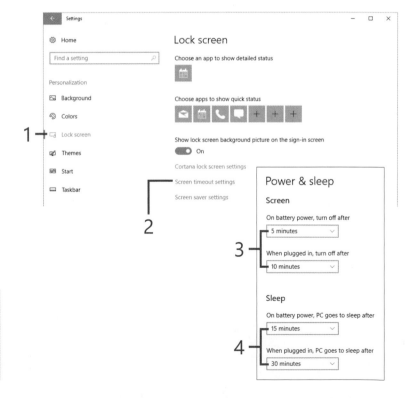

> ⚠ **CAUTION** Setting up too long an interval before your computer turns off the screen or goes to sleep can drain a laptop battery. Default settings are often suitable for most people, but if you do choose a lengthier interval, you should be aware of your power consumption trade-offs.

# Enlarging text

If you want Windows interface text to be displayed in a larger size to help you read things more easily, you can use a System setting to choose a new text size. This setting affects the text in Windows elements: dialog boxes, Settings windows, the taskbar, the Start menu, and so forth. It does not control text size in individual apps.

## Make text larger

1 In Settings, choose System, and then click Display.

2 Go to the Scale and Layout section, pull down the Change the Size of Text, Apps, and Other Items list, and select the setting you desire.

3 To select a different size for text and other items, click Custom Scaling and enter a custom amount.

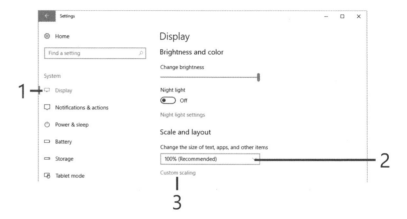

**TRY THIS** If you have a touchscreen computer, you can use your fingers to expand or reduce the display of many apps, including the Microsoft Edge browser. To enlarge the display, simply put two fingers together on the screen and spread them apart. To reduce the size of the display, place your fingers apart and pinch them toward each other.

**TIP** If you have vision issues, use the Magnifier Ease of Access feature to zoom in on areas of your screen; it works as if you're holding a magnifying glass to the screen. See "Using Magnifier" on page 90 for more about using this feature.

# Changing screen resolution

The monitor on your computer or laptop displays your desktop and its contents at a certain resolution, expressed in pixels in a ratio of height to width, such as 1366 x 768. Resolutions containing higher numbers provide a crisper screen, though onscreen elements might be smaller. Resolutions with a lower number provide a less crisp image, but onscreen elements are larger, which might make the screen more readable for some. If you ever share images of your desktop, you might be asked to shoot those images at a certain resolution, so it's useful to know how to change this setting.

## Choose a screen resolution

1   In Settings, choose System, and then click Display.

2   Click the Resolution drop-down list, and then select the setting you want.

---

**TIP**   Not all computers offer the same resolution options, because these depend on the individual monitor used. Newer computers with higher-quality displays and better-quality graphics cards will typically offer higher resolution settings.

**TIP**   If you have a notebook computer, most manufacturers have a recommended screen resolution that will appear as such in the Resolution drop-down list. Choose this setting for the best display.

# Customizing the taskbar

You can customize the taskbar that runs along the bottom of the Windows desktop in several ways. First, you can control whether the taskbar is locked in place so that it can't shift to a different position. You can also control whether your taskbar is automatically hidden so that you can view the full screen without it until you move your pointing device near its position on the screen. You can move the taskbar to the top, bottom, right, or left of the screen. You can also change which Quick Action buttons, such as those that control volume, power, network connections, and so forth, appear on the right side of the taskbar.

## Choose taskbar settings

1   Right-click the taskbar.

2   Click Taskbar Settings.

3   Click on any of the settings switches, such as Lock the Taskbar or Automatically Hide the Taskbar in Desktop Mode, to apply that setting.

*(continued on next page)*

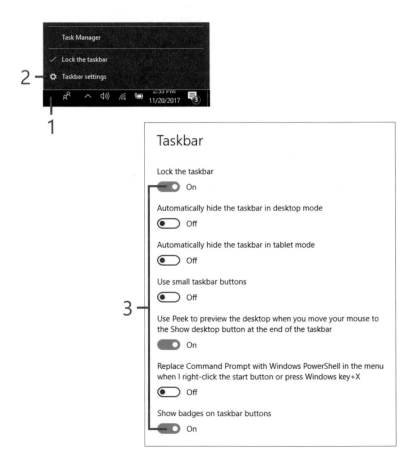

## Choose taskbar settings *continued*

**4** Scroll down to and click the Taskbar Location On Screen drop-down box and click a location.

**5** To change which icons appear on the taskbar, scroll to the Notification Area section, and click Select Which Icons Appear on the Taskbar.

**6** Move the slider to the On or Off position next to each individual icon listed.

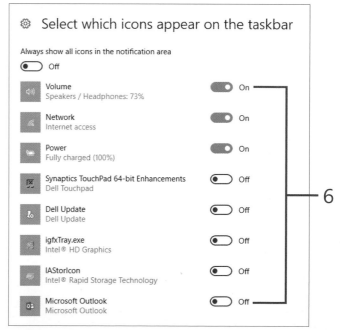

# Adding tiles to the Start menu

There are several apps tiles included in the Start menu when you first turn on your Windows 10 computer. In designing Windows 10, Microsoft bet that these would be the most commonly used and useful tiles, but you can also choose which apps you prefer to pin to the Start menu.

## Add a new tile to the Start menu

**1** Click the Start button.

**2** Right-click an app in the apps list.

**3** Click Pin to Start.

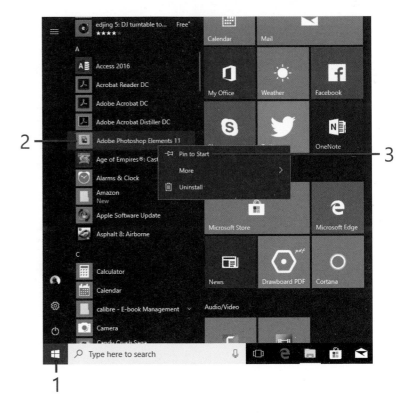

**TIP** Don't need an app tile on your Start menu anymore? You can remove an app tile by right-clicking it in the Start menu, and then, in the shortcut menu that opens, click Unpin From Start.

# Moving tiles

The position of a tile on your Start menu can make it easier to find. For example, you might want to place your most commonly used app tiles along the top, and less-used tiles at the bottom.

Or, you might decide to move a tile from one group of tiles to another. You can easily move tiles around on the Start menu by dragging them from place to place.

## Move a tile

**1** Click the Start button.

**2** Click and drag a tile to a new location on the Start menu, and then release the mouse button.

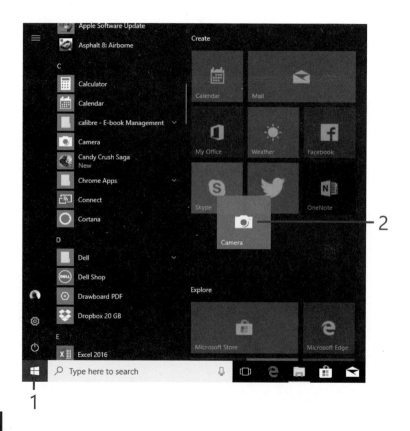

**TRY THIS** When you add tiles to the Start menu, they appear in a new group. Add a couple of tiles and then click above them and type a name for the new group. Try moving a tile from one group to another using the procedure described here.

# Using Snap to arrange apps on the desktop

Snap is a feature that has been around for several versions of Windows. Snap helps you to quickly arrange open windows on the right or left side of your screen. Windows 10 adds a vertical snap functionality that makes it possible for you to move an open but not maximized app window to the top or bottom of your screen. The Snap feature works by selecting an app and dragging it, by using shortcut keys, or, with a touchscreen, by swiping an open app with your finger.

## Snap apps

**1** Using the Start menu, open several apps on the desktop.

**2** Click the title bar of an open app and quickly drag it to the left side of the screen.

*(continued on next page)*

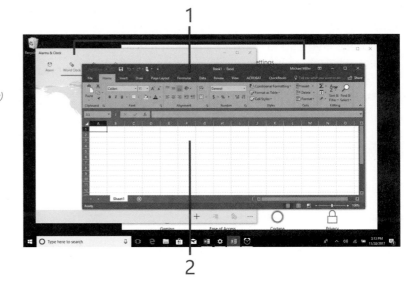

## Snap apps   *continued*

**3**  Thumbnails for other apps now appear on the right side of the screen. Click a thumbnail to snap this app to the right of the first app.

**4**  The two apps now display side-by-side, each taking up half the screen. Click and drag the border between the two apps to resize the two of them.

3

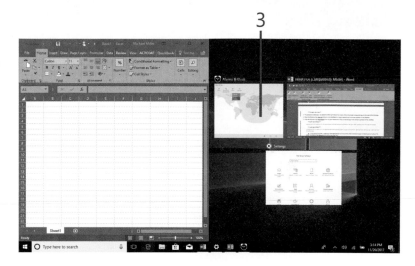

4

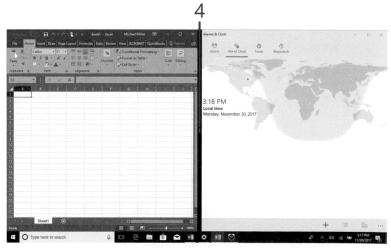

  **TIP**  If you have a touchscreen, dragging an open app's title bar to the top of the screen maximizes the app.

# Resizing tiles

Your Start menu can become crowded with tiles as you continue to add apps to it. One way to relieve the clutter and view more tiles in the menu is to reduce the size of some tiles. You might also want to enlarge a tile that you want to more easily find. There are four sizes for tiles: Small, Medium, Wide, and Large.

## Change tile size

1 Click the Start button.

2 Right-click a tile.

3 Click Resize

4 Click Small, Medium, Wide, or Large.

---

**TIP**   You might have noticed that some tiles have specific content such as a news story displayed on them, whereas others only sport a solid background and an icon. Tiles with content in them are called *live tiles*. If the live content in a tile distracts you, right-click that app tile in the Start menu, and then, in the shortcut menu that opens, choose Turn Live Tile Off.

# Working with productivity applications

# 5

These days, there is an app for just about anything, but many of these are small programs with limited functionality, such as a to-do list or calculator app. More robust applications (often used in a business setting, such as a word processor or database) incorporate more complex functionality. For example, you might work with text, numbers, images, and the ability to produce a graph, report, or slide show in a single application.

These full-featured products are called *productivity applications*. When you open such applications, you find that many share certain features, such as the ability to format text in several ways and to cut, copy, and paste items from one document to another or from one location in a document to another. You complete many actions in productivity software by using a combination of toolbars and menus. When you finish creating a document, you can save it, print it, or share it. You might use these applications in the cloud, as with Microsoft Office 365, or they might be installed on your computer. Knowing how to use some basic functionality of productivity applications in Windows 10 will help you get up to speed when you encounter a new application.

## In this section:

- Finding and opening applications using the Start menu
- Opening applications using Cortana
- Working with toolbars and menus
- Cutting, copying, and pasting content
- Formatting text
- Formatting paragraphs
- Saving files
- Printing documents
- Sharing files via email
- Closing applications
- Uninstalling applications

# Finding and opening applications using the Start menu

The best way to find and open applications in Windows 10 is by using the Start menu. This menu offers a choice among the applications you use most, a list of all installed applications, and tiles that provide a visual way to access applications. Many tiles can be *live*—meaning that they show updated content from the Internet or computer, as with the Weather and Calendar apps.

## Open an application using the Start menu

**1** Click the Start button.

**2** In the Apps list, scroll down (if necessary) and click an application to open it.

**3** Alternatively, click the tile for the app you want to open.

✅ **TIP** Note that in the lower-left corner of the Start menu are buttons for your user account, Settings, and Power that you can use to access these frequently used features.

# Opening applications using Cortana

You can use Cortana beyond just searching for information. She also performs certain actions on command, such as playing music or setting up a reminder. One useful feature of Cortana is her ability to open applications. You can ask Cortana to open an application just by asking her, or, in the Cortana search box, you can type **open** followed by the application name.

## Ask Cortana to open an application

1   Click the Cortana search box.

2   Type the phrase **open** *app*, replacing *app* with the name of the app you want to open, such as WordPad.

3   The desired app should be listed at the top of Cortana's search results. Press Enter on your keyboard.

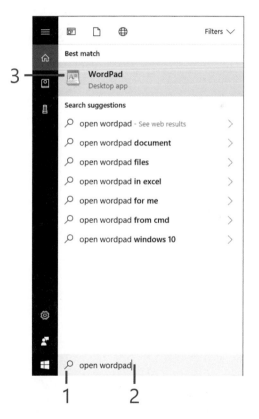

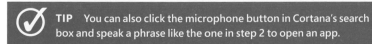
**TIP**   You can also click the microphone button in Cortana's search box and speak a phrase like the one in step 2 to open an app.

# Working with toolbars and menus

A common element in most productivity applications is the use of tools and menus. Tools are icons arranged on a toolbar or, in the case of Microsoft productivity applications, a *ribbon*. Toolbars often include tabs that you click to display a different set of tools. For example, in WordPad (included with Windows 10), the

ribbon includes File, Home, and View tabs. These tabs break the tools into logical groups to help you find what you need. Some productivity applications also use menus with drop-down lists of commands that you can choose.

## Use tools and menu commands

1  Open WordPad (see the previous task).

2  On the ribbon, click the View tab.

3  Clear the Ruler check box to remove the ruler from the screen.

4  Click the File tab.

5  Click Page Setup.

6  Click the Landscape option in the Page Setup dialog box.

7  Click OK.

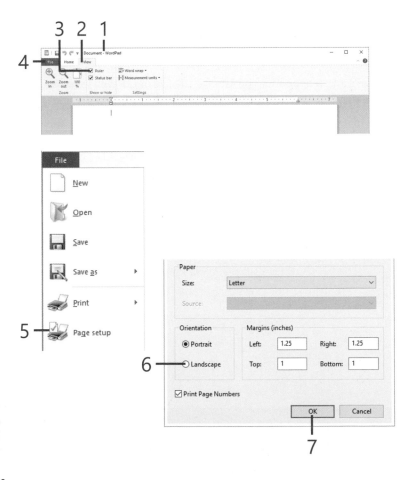

> ✓ **TIP**  In Microsoft productivity applications such as Word or Excel, the ribbon sometimes contains a small arrow at the lower-right corner of a group of tools (for example, the Font group on the Home tab in Word). You can click this arrow to open a dialog box in which you can configure several Font settings in one place. Dialog boxes often offer a few more advanced settings than are available on the toolbars.

# Cutting, copying, and pasting content

One useful function you'll find in productivity and other applications is the ability to cut, copy, and paste text and objects. You can perform these actions within a single document, or you can cut or copy content in one document and paste it into another.

Cut removes content from the original location, whereas Copy makes a duplicate of the content but leaves the original in place. The Cut, Copy, and Paste tools make use of the Windows Clipboard, which is a holding place for cut or copied content.

## Cut, copy, and paste

1 With WordPad open, type a sentence.

2 Click and drag your mouse pointer across the sentence to select it.

3 On the ribbon, on the Home tab, click the Cut (or Copy) button.

4 Position the cursor where you want to paste the text, and then, on the ribbon, click the Paste button.

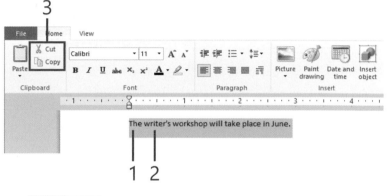

> ✓ **TIP** When you cut or copy something, it stays in the Clipboard until you cut or copy something else. You can paste the latest content of the Clipboard as many times as you like until it's replaced.

> ✓ **TIP** When you paste content, you might see a small icon at the end of the pasted item. Click this to choose paste options. For example, you might choose to retain the original formatting or apply the formatting in the new document to the pasted text.

# Formatting text

Whether you're working in a database, a spreadsheet, a slide presentation application, or a word processor, it's likely that you'll add text to your document. You can format text in various ways; for example, by applying a different font, choosing a different color, or making the text bold or italic. Formatting text can make it look more appealing, professional, or even quirky, depending on the kind of document you're creating. You can use the Font tools in most applications to make formatting changes.

## Apply formatting to text

1  With WordPad open, type this sentence: We're experiencing unusually warm weather this year.

2  Drag the mouse pointer to select the entire sentence.

3  On the ribbon, on the Home tab, click the Font drop-down list.

4  Click to select Book Antiqua.

5  Select the word unusually.

6  On the ribbon, (on the Home tab) click the Underline button.

7  Click the Text Color drop-down list, and then select the color red from the palette.

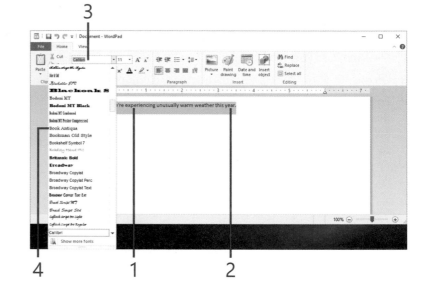

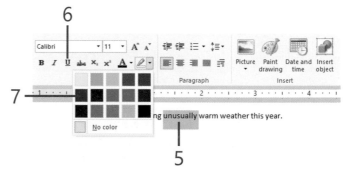

# Formatting paragraphs

Many documents include sentences arranged in paragraphs. You can format paragraphs to add spacing between sentences within the paragraph and between the paragraphs themselves. You can indent the first line of a paragraph or the entire paragraph, as when citing a long quote. You can also align text in paragraphs to the left or right, or centered on the page. Finally, you can format a paragraph as a list with numbers or bullets.

## Apply formatting to paragraphs

**1** Open a document in WordPad or create a new document and type a paragraph.

**2** Select the paragraph.

**3** On the ribbon, on the Home tab, click the Line Spacing drop-down list, and then select 2.

**4** Click the Increase Indent button.

**5** Click the Start a List button.

**TRY THIS** Many standard letter and report formats require that the first line of a paragraph be indented. On the WordPad ribbon, click the Paragraph button. In the dialog box that opens, click the First Line indentation box, and increase the indentation to 1.

# Saving files

By saving a document, you can continue working on it in the future or open it and review it or share it with others. When you save a document, you give it a name, and you can then open it from the originating application, or by locating it in File Explorer.

You can organize saved files in folders that you name in a way that makes items easy to locate later. The first time you save a file, you'll use the Save command. If you want to save a file with a new name, use the Save As command.

## Save a file

**1** With a new document open in an application such as WordPad, click File.

**2** Click Save.

**3** On the left side of the Save As dialog box, browse through the folders to find the location where you want to save the file.

**4** In the File Name box, type a name.

**5** If you want to save the file in a particular format, click the Save as Type drop-down list, and then select the format.

**6** Click the Save button.

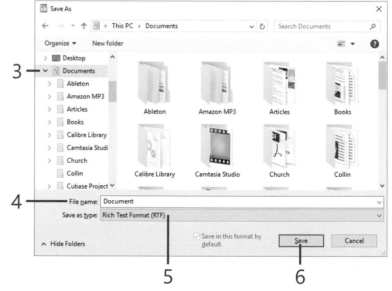

> ✓ **TIP** Don't wait until you're done working on a document to save it. If you don't save your changes every now and then while you're working, you risk losing the changes you've added. Though many applications have autosave features to save your files for you, to be absolutely sure, you should manually save your work every 5 or 10 minutes.

# Printing documents

Although we live in a world that has been called "paperless," the fact is that we often need to print a hard copy of a document or image. Printing works much the same way from one productivity application to another, though the choices might vary based on your printer model and manufacturer. For example, color options won't be available if your device prints only in black and white. Options commonly available include the number of copies; whether you want copies collated; orientation and size of the paper; whether to print in black and white, color, or grayscale; which range of pages in the document to print; and so on.

## Print a document

1 With a document open in an application such as WordPad, click File.

2 Click Print.

3 In the list that displays on the right, click Print.

4 Select the printer to which you want to send your pages.

5 Select the number of copies.

6 Select the range of pages to print.

7 Click Print.

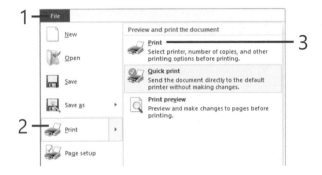

> **TIP** A shortcut to open the Print dialog box is to press Ctrl+P on your keyboard. There are some instances when a formal Print command isn't easy to find (for example on some sites on the web). In those situations, knowing this shortcut can prove invaluable.

# Sharing files via email

Today, via the Internet, there are several ways to share documents with others, from sending them by email to creating an online presentation. The options you're offered for sharing depend on the application you're using. For example, with Microsoft PowerPoint, you can publish slides as an online presentation, and with Word, you can post a document on a blog.

For all applications on a Windows computer, you can save files to Microsoft OneDrive, an online file-sharing service. WordPad has less-sophisticated sharing features, but you can send a document via Outlook email (you need to have or set up an Outlook email account before performing these steps).

## Share a document via email

1   With a WordPad document open, click File.

2   Click Send In Email.

3   In the To box, type an email address.

4   In the Subject box, type a topic.

5   Type a message.

6   Click Send.

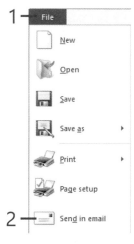

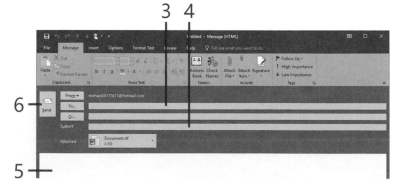

**TIP**   To save a file to OneDrive, click the File menu, click Save As, and then browse to locate OneDrive on your computer. This saves a copy of the document to your local OneDrive folder, which synchronizes periodically with the online OneDrive service. You can then share those documents with others from OneDrive.

# Closing applications

When you're done working with an application for a time, although you can leave it running, you might want to close it. With fewer applications running, you free up some of your computer's memory, which improves performance. Closing an application is easy.

## Close an open application

**1** With an application open, first save any open document.

**2** Click the Close button.

 **TIP** You can also click the File menu and then choose the Close or Exit command to close most applications.

# Uninstalling applications

If you no longer need an application on your computer, you can uninstall it. However, if there's a chance that you might need the application again someday, be sure that you have it either on disk or you have a product key for downloading the application from the Internet.

## Remove an application from your computer

1 Click the Start button.

2 Click Settings.

3 Click Apps.

4 Make sure Apps & Features is selected.

5 Click a program in the list.

6 Click the Uninstall button.

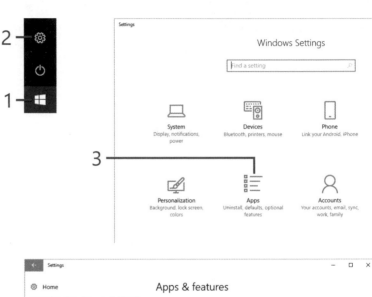

> ✓ **TIP** Depending on the application you're uninstalling, it might simply uninstall at this point, or Windows might ask you to confirm whether to uninstall by clicking a button labeled Finish or something similar. Some application suites—such as Office, which contains several applications—might ask you to choose which application to remove. Just respond to any prompts to finish the uninstall process.

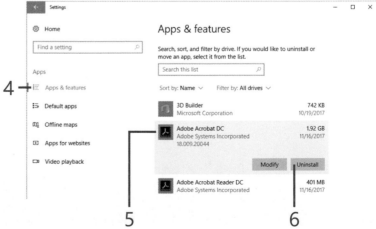

# Finding content with File Explorer and Cortana

# 6

File Explorer is the feature of Windows with which you can locate and organize the files saved on your computer and on external media such as USB sticks or DVD drives. File Explorer organizes content using a hierarchy of files saved within folders and subfolders.

Also, you can use the new personal assistant, Cortana, to find files and folders on your computer as well as information and content stored online. Using these two features of Windows, you can locate everything, from a single file saved on your computer to the virtually infinite content available on the Internet.

## In this section:

- Finding content with File Explorer
- Changing File Explorer views
- Sorting files
- Creating a new folder
- Moving files among folders
- Renaming files or folders
- Deleting files or folders
- Compressing files
- Sharing files via email
- Managing the Recycle Bin
- Searching with Cortana
- Searching for favorite places

# Finding content with File Explorer

When you save files in Windows, you can create folders and place files within those folders to organize the files. File Explorer is like a table of contents for your computer's contents. When you open File Explorer, you can choose a drive, such as your computer's hard disk or a USB stick (or even Microsoft's OneDrive online storage service), move through its contents by selecting a folder—perhaps a subfolder—and then individual files. Using File Explorer, you can view a variety of information about files, such as the date they were last updated, their author, or their file size.

## Locate files and folders

1   On the taskbar or Start menu, click the File Explorer icon.

2   In the left panel, click a folder.

3   In the right pane, double-click a subfolder, if one exists. (Or, in the left panel, single-click a subfolder.)

4   Double-click a file to open it.

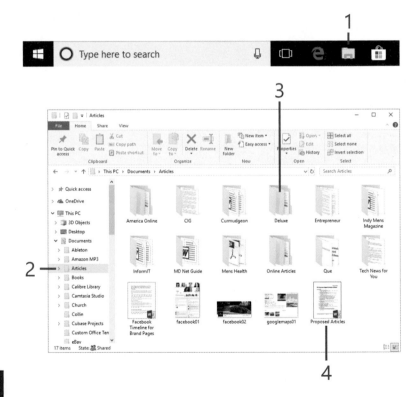

**→  TRY THIS**   You can use the Search feature in File Explorer to locate a file. With File Explorer open, click the Search box, and then type a file or folder name. Double-click an item in the results to open it.

# Changing File Explorer views

People like to view information in different ways or with different levels of detail. In File Explorer, you can choose to see a list of files and folders or icons of various sizes that represent the items.

You can also choose to view a preview of a selected file or details about it such as its author, size, and the last date and time it was modified and saved.

## Change views

1 Open File Explorer and then double-click a folder (such as Pictures) to open it.

2 On the ribbon, click the View tab.

3 In the Layout group, click List.

4 In the Panes group, click Details Pane.

5 Click a file to display its details in the right pane.

*(continued on next page)*

---

**TIP** You can use the Show/Hide check boxes toward the right side of the View tab on the ribbon to show or hide elements or information such as check boxes to the left of files and folders in a list, file name extensions (such as .exe), hidden items, or items you've selected.

## Change views *continued*

6 In the Panes group, click Preview Pane.

7 In the Layout group, click Medium Icons.

8 Click a file to display a preview of that file in the right pane.

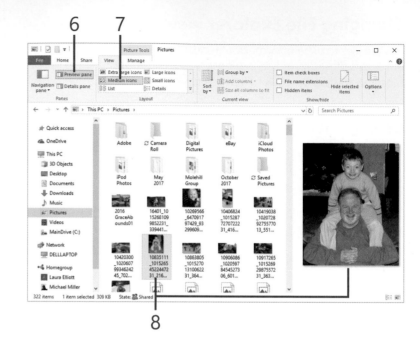

# Sorting files

Being able to sort files by various criteria can help you spot the file you need. For example, if you have a file named Vacation-March and another named Vacation-Islands that contain similar information, you might want to find the latest saved version or the one that's of a certain file type. With File Explorer, you can sort files by several criteria to help you locate just what you need.

## Sort files

1 With File Explorer open, double-click a folder to open it.

2 Click a file and then, on the ribbon, on the View tab, click Details Pane.

3 Click Sort By.

4 Click to select criteria such as Date or Size.

# Creating a new folder

Folders are the way to organize your files in Windows, just as you place papers related to a particular project in a physical folder. You can use some folders that Windows provides out of the box, such as Documents and Pictures, or you can create your own folders. You can also create subfolders; for example, a construction project folder might contain subfolders for cost quotes, building plans, and correspondence.

## Create a new folder

1 With File Explorer open, click the folder within which you want to create the new folder. For example, you could click the Documents folder to create a subfolder within it.

2 On the ribbon, click the Home tab.

3 Click New Folder.

4 Type a name for the new folder.

5 Click anywhere outside the new folder to save the new name.

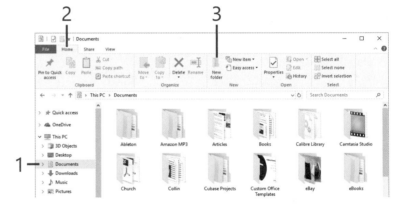

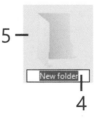

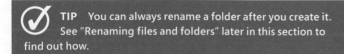

> **TIP** You can always rename a folder after you create it. See "Renaming files and folders" later in this section to find out how.

# Moving files among folders

There are times when you might choose to move a file from one folder to another. Or, perhaps you want to place a copy of a file in another folder. For example, you might have a file containing a local caterer's menu that you keep in a restaurant menus folder, but you also want to place a copy in your daughter's wedding plans folder. You can either move a file from one location to another using the Cut button or make a copy of it using the Copy button to have it available in both locations.

## Move or copy one file to another location

1   With File Explorer open, click to select the file you want to move or copy.

2   On the ribbon, on the Home tab, click Copy (to make a copy of the file) or Cut (to move the file).

3   In the left pane, locate the folder to which you want to move or copy the file and click it.

4   Click the Paste button.

> **TIP**   You can also drag a file or folder from one displayed folder to another folder in the left pane of the File Explorer window. However, be aware that this moves the file or folder to the new location, removing it from the original location.

# Renaming files and folders

We tend to name files and folders on the fly, not always thinking of the most appropriate name. Occasionally, you'll want to rename a file or folder more accurately so that you can find it faster or to differentiate it from another item. You can rename files and folders as many times as you like.

## Rename a file or folder

1   In File Explorer, click to select the file or folder you wish to rename.

2   On the Home tab, click Rename.

3   In the text box that opens, type a name for the file or folder.

4   Click anywhere outside the text box to save the new name.

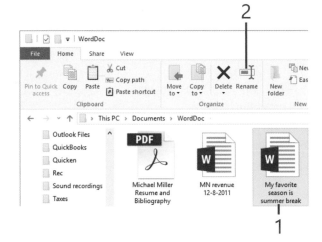

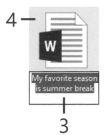

 **TIP** You can also rename a file by selecting it and then pressing F2 on your keyboard.

# Deleting files and folders

When you've archived an older file or folder on a storage medium, or you simply no longer need the item, you can delete it. Deleting old files not only clears some space on your computer's storage device, but it also makes folders easier to navigate when using File Explorer.

## Delete a file or folder

1  With File Explorer open, on the ribbon, click the Home tab.

2  Click the item.

3  On the ribbon, in the Organize group, click Delete.

**CAUTION**  Windows does not confirm the deletion of a file or folder, so be sure that you really want to delete it before clicking the Delete button. (You can, however, undo a deletion by immediately pressing Ctrl+Z.)

**TIP**  You can also delete an item by selecting it and then pressing Delete on your computer keyboard.

# Compressing files

Although you can use an online sharing service such as OneDrive to store and share even large files easily, sometimes you might want to compress a file (also called *zipping*) to be able to attach it to an email or store it using less space. Compressing reduces the file size, making it easier to transmit to others who can then *unzip* the file on their computers.

## Compress files into a zip folder

1   With File Explorer open, click the first file you want to compress and then, while holding down the Shift key on your keyboard, click the last file in the series. Alternatively, click the first file to select it, then hold down the Ctrl key to select the other files.

2   On the ribbon, click the Share tab.

3   In the Send group, click Zip.

4   In the text box that opens, type a name for the compressed file.

5   Click anywhere outside the text box to save the name.

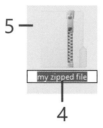

> **TIP** You should have all the files that you want to compress stored in the same folder on your computer. If the files are in the same folder but not adjacent to one another, click the first file, and then, with the Ctrl key pressed, continue to click additional files. When all the files are selected, continue with step 2.

# Sharing files via email

Who hasn't taken a picture or written a poem that they want to instantly share with others? Windows 10 offers many ways to share content, including by email or the Skype messaging service. File Explorer includes its own Share tab on the ribbon that offers the necessary tools for sharing your content with others.

## Send a file via email

1 With File Explorer open, locate and select a file that you want to share.

2 On the ribbon, click the Share tab.

3 In the Send group, click Share.

4 In the Share panel, click Mail.

*(continued on next page)*

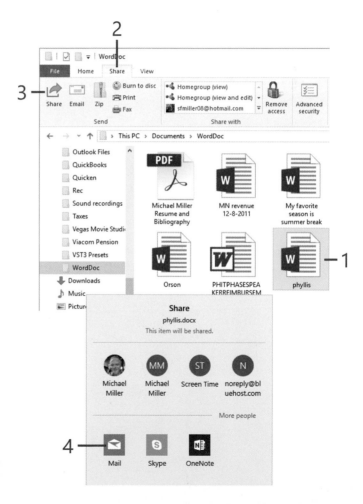

> **TIP** You can also share a file via Skype. Select the file in File Explorer, select the Share tab, and then click Share. When the Sharing pane appears, click Skype; this opens the Skype app. Enter an accompanying text message if you want, and then select the person or group to which you want to send the file.

## Send a file via email *continued*

**5** Fill out the Email form with an addressee, subject, and message.

**6** Click Send.

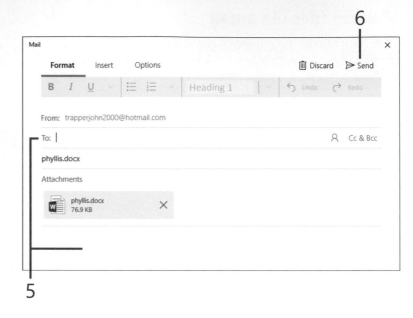

# Searching with Cortana

Cortana is touted as a personal assistant, and she can indeed perform a variety of actions. However, one of the main roles of Cortana is to act as a search tool, giving you the means to search both for items on your computer and items online. You can find Cortana on the taskbar, and she provides you with two ways to search: by voice command or by typing a search term using your keyboard.

## Search with Cortana

1  On the taskbar, click the Cortana search box.

2  Type a search word or phrase.

3  To narrow your search results, click the Filters down arrow and make a selection, such as Documents or Folders.

4  Click a result to open that item.

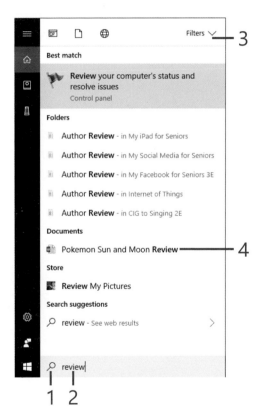

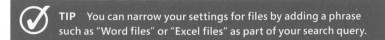

**TIP** You can narrow your settings for files by adding a phrase such as "Word files" or "Excel files" as part of your search query.

# Searching for favorite places

You can use the Favorite Places feature of Cortana to search for and save locations such as nearby restaurants and movie theaters. Cortana searches for a list of favorites, and you can then save an item in your Favorites list so that you can access it easily in the future. Note that to achieve the most accurate results for local establishments, you should turn on the Location feature in the Action Center.

## Find and add favorite places

1   Click in the Cortana search box.

2   Click the Notebook button.

3   Click About Me.

4   Click Edit Favorites.

5   Click the Add (+) button.

*(continued on next page)*

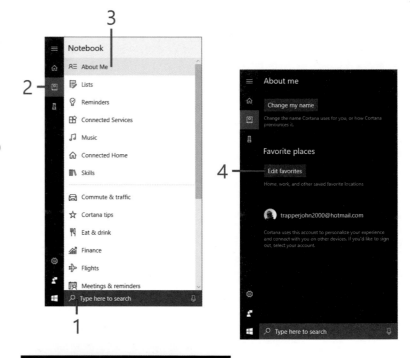

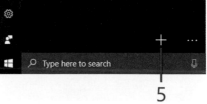

## Find and add favorite places  *continued*

**6** In the Add a Favorite box, type a term.

**7** Click a result.

**8** Type a nickname, if you like.

**9** Click the Set As Home or Set As Work settings to turn one on so that requests to Cortana for directions, weather, and so on can be answered based on the appropriate location.

**10** Click Save.

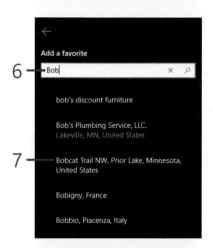

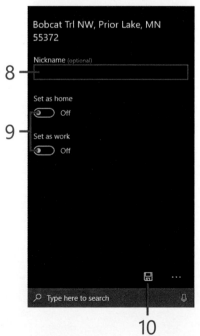

○ **TIP** To get a map to a location, open Favorite Places in Cortana, and then click Directions under a location. If asked, permit Cortana to access your current location. Cortana opens the Maps app and displays directions for you. For more about using the Maps app, see Section 19, "Using Maps."

# Managing the Recycle Bin

When you delete a file or folder, it's sent to the Recycle Bin—a kind of trash can that holds your deleted content until it becomes so full that it destroys older contents. Even after you delete an item, you can often use the Recycle Bin to locate and restore it to its folder. The Recycle Bin is essentially a folder in File Explorer, which provides a Manage tab on the ribbon for managing Recycle Bin contents.

## Restore an item from the Recycle Bin

**1** From the desktop, double-click the Recycle Bin.

**2** Click the Manage tab if it's not already displayed.

**3** Click an item in the folder.

**4** On the Ribbon, on the Manage tab, click Restore the Selected Items.

> ✓ **TIP** To restore all items in the Recycle Bin, click Restore All Items in the Restore group of the Manage tab. You can also permanently empty the Recycle Bin of all contents by clicking Empty Recycle Bin.

# Making Windows accessible

# 7

Windows is used by millions of people around the globe. Some of those people face challenges in using a computer. Some have dexterity issues such as carpal tunnel syndrome or arthritis and need to adjust mouse and keyboard settings to make providing input easier. Others face visual challenges that make content on the screen difficult to read. Some might need help hearing sounds or require an alternative way to connect with the spoken word in videos, such as closed captioning.

Windows 10 offers several accessibility features to address these needs, such as Magnifier to enlarge content on the screen, Narrator to read content to a user, the ability to adjust screen brightness or contrast, and the option of speaking text rather than typing it. These tools make using a Windows 10 computer very easy.

## In this section:

- Using Magnifier
- Setting up high contrast
- Using a color filter for color blindness
- Adjusting screen brightness
- Making elements on your screen easier to see
- Changing mouse settings
- Changing keyboard settings
- Using Touch Feedback
- Working with Narrator
- Turning on Closed Captioning
- Using Speech Recognition
- Using visual alternatives for sounds

# Using Magnifier

Although it's possible to enlarge or reduce contents for individual apps and tools—such as on a webpage or in a word-processing document—it's not possible to enlarge the Windows environment itself. For example, you can't enlarge the entire desktop (though you can enlarge the icons for desktop shortcuts).

To view the entire on-screen environment at a significantly larger size, you use Windows 10's Magnifier feature. Magnifier works much like a magnifying glass on your computer screen and is useful to those who have poor vision.

## Turn on Magnifier

1 Click the Start button.

2 Click Settings.

3 Click Ease of Access.

4 Click Magnifier.

5 Click to turn on Magnifier.

6 In the Magnifier controls, click the Zoom In button to zoom in.

7 Click the Zoom Out button to zoom out.

8 Click the Close button to close Magnifier and return to normal viewing.

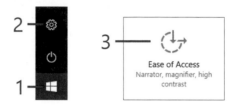

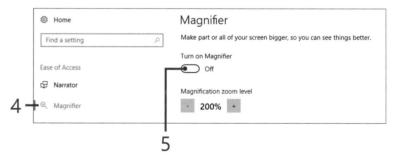

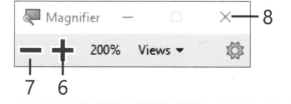

> **TRY THIS** For some people, a dark background with white text is easier to read. To invert color to make the screen black and text white, click Magnifier in the Ease of Access settings, turn on Magnifier, and then check the Invert Colors option.

> **TIP** If you have a touchscreen computer, you can also zoom in or out in Magnifier by pinching in or spreading out with two fingers on the screen.

> **TIP** After a few seconds, the Magnifier controls change to a magnifying glass icon. To redisplay the controls, click the magnifying glass.

# Setting up high contrast

You can make elements on your screen easier to discern if you increase the contrast between lighter and darker colored objects. To do that, you can apply any of four preset high-contrast color schemes. These schemes control the color of your background, selected text, hyperlinks, and more.

## Make high-contrast settings

**1**  In the Ease of Access settings window, click Color & High Contrast.

**2**  Click the Choose a Theme drop-down list and click a theme.

**3**  Click Apply.

✓ **TIP**  If you have difficulty discerning colors, choose a high-contrast theme that contains colors you can easily see.

# Using a color filter for color blindness

If you are color blind, you may find it difficult to distinguish similar-colored elements onscreen. The Windows 10 Fall Creators Update adds a color filter option that displays colors in shades of gray or other colors that may be easier for you to see.

## Apply a color filter

1 In the Ease of Access settings window, click Color & High Contrast.

2 In the Color Filters section, click the Apply Color Filter switch to turn on the feature.

3 Open the drop-down list for Choose a Filter and make a selection.

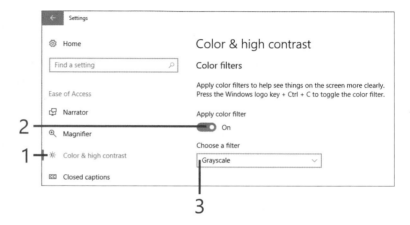

 **TIP**   You can activate the selected color filter at any time by pressing Windows+Ctrl+C.

## Adjusting screen brightness

The brightness setting for your screen can make elements on the screen easier to see. However, be aware that if you're using a laptop, the brighter you set your screen, the quicker you'll drain your battery.

### Set the screen to be brighter or dimmer

**1**  Click the Action Center button.

**2**  Click the Brightness button.

**3**  Click the button again to move to the next highest brightness level in increments of 25 percent.

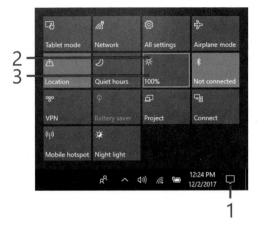

---

TIP   If you have a notebook PC, you can also go to the System settings window and click Display to access a brightness slider. This slider gives you much greater control over the increments of brightness on your screen.

## Making elements on your screen easier to see

You can adjust some visual options to help you spot certain elements on your screen. For example, you can adjust the thickness of your mouse pointer (the little arrow on the screen that shows the location of your mouse). You can also control the duration that notifications about your computer, such as how to handle a newly inserted USB stick, stay on the screen, to give you more time to read them.

### Adjust how cursors and notifications appear

1 In the Ease of Access settings window, click Other Options on the left.

2 Click the Show Notifications For arrow and select an increment from 5 seconds to 5 minutes.

3 Click the Cursor Thickness slider and drag it to the desired width.

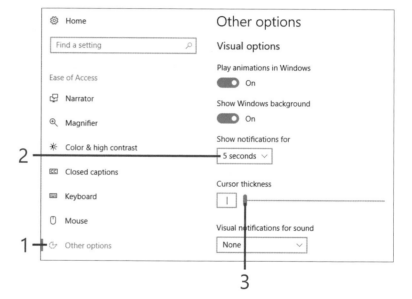

**TIP** If it's easier for you to make out items on the desktop with no background showing, you can turn off the Show Windows Background setting in the Visual options section shown here. This turns your desktop background to black.

# Changing mouse settings

Whether your mouse control comes from a touchpad or moveable mouse, when you use it around your screen, it displays a variety of symbols often called *pointers*. You can control the size and color of your mouse pointer in the Ease of Access settings, and even configure it so that keys on your numeric keypad can control the movement of your pointer on the screen if you have trouble controlling a physical mouse device. When this feature is turned on, numeric keypads embedded in keyboards have keys that you can use to move the pointer up, down, left, and right, as well as paging up and down.

## Change how your mouse works

1 In the Ease of Access settings window, click Mouse on the left side.

2 Click to select a pointer size.

3 Click to select the pointer color (white, black, or white and black).

4 Click to turn the numeric keypad mouse control on or off.

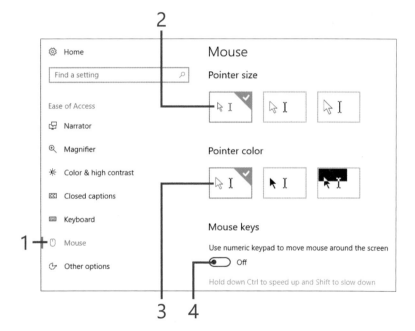

TIP   When you turn on the numeric keypad to control the mouse, you can also use two other settings to press and hold the Ctrl key to speed up mouse functionality or use the mouse keys only when the Num Lock setting is set to on for your keyboard.

# Changing keyboard settings

Using a keyboard can present certain challenges. If you have arthritis or other conditions that present dexterity issues, pressing two shortcut keys at once can be difficult. In that case, you can use Sticky Keys to allow for pressing one key at a time when entering a shortcut on your keyboard. Also, we've all pressed a key like Caps Lock without realizing it. In the Ease of Access settings window, you can turn on Toggle Keys, a feature that has your computer make a sound when you press Caps Lock, Num Lock, or Scroll Lock. Finally, Filter Keys is a feature that causes Windows 10 to disregard a brief or repeated key press. If you have dexterity challenges, this can be useful to avoid unintended entries.

## Specify how you interact with your keyboard

1   In the Ease of Access settings window, click Keyboard.

2   Click the switch to turn on Sticky Keys.

3   Click the switch to turn on Toggle Keys.

4   Click the switch to turn on Filter Keys.

> ✓ **TIP**   If you want to know if you've turned on or off a setting by pressing a shortcut key combination, scroll down to the Other Settings section of the Keyboard page and click the switches to turn on either (or both): Display a Warning Message When Turning a Setting On With a Shortcut or Make a Sound When Turning a Setting On Or Off With a Shortcut

# Using touch feedback

If you have a touchscreen computer, you will often touch the screen to select a feature or even to draw. Touch Feedback displays a pale circle when you touch the screen, providing you with visual feedback that your tap was recognized. You can turn Touch Feedback on or off; also, you can turn on a setting to provide a more enhanced visual feedback on your screen.

## Get feedback from your touchscreen

**1** In the Ease of Access settings window, click Other Options.

**2** The Show Visual Feedback When I Touch the Screen setting is turned on by default. Click the switch to turn it on if the setting has been switched off.

**3** Click the Use Darker, Larger Visual Feedback switch to turn it on.

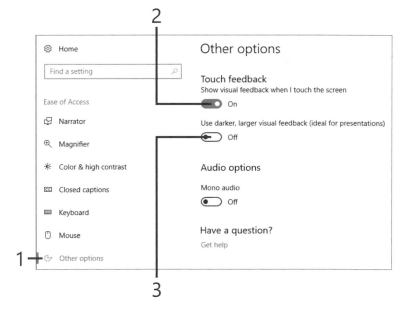

---

✓ **TIP**   You must turn on the Show Visual Feedback When I Touch The Screen setting before you can access the setting to make the feedback darker.

# Working with Narrator

If you have difficulty seeing what's on your screen, you might want to investigate the Narrator feature. Using Narrator, Windows can "speak," telling you what is currently displayed on the screen, describing items such as text and buttons. When you turn on the Narrator feature, you must click an element on the screen, such as an item in Settings to hear details about it, and then click it again to activate it.

## Turn on Narrator

1 In the Ease of Access settings window, in the left pane, click Narrator.

2 Click the Narrator switch to turn on the feature.

3 Click the Start Narrator Automatically switch to turn on Narrator whenever you log in to Windows 10.

4 Click the arrow to open the Choose a Voice list, and then select one of the available male or female voices.

5 Click anywhere in the Speed setting to speed up the Narrator speech.

6 Click anywhere in the Pitch setting to adjust the pitch of the Narrator's voice from lower to higher.

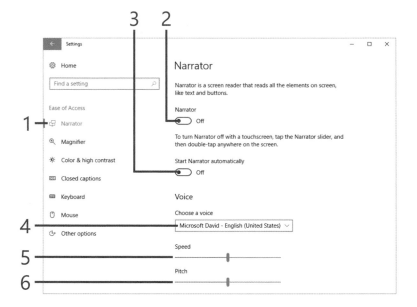

> **TIP** You can configure additional Narrator settings in the Ease of Access settings window. For example, you can set which elements that you want Narrator to read, such as words you type and hints for buttons. You also have the option of highlighting mouse pointers, insertion points, and keys on a touch keyboard when you lift your finger from them.

# Turning on closed captioning

If you are hard of hearing, you might have used the closed-captioning feature on a television so that you could read what's being said. Your Windows computer also has a closed captioning feature, and you can set up the color, transparency, font style, and size of the captions in the Ease Of Access settings window.

## Choose closed captions options

1   In the Ease of Access settings window, in the left pane, click Closed Captions.

2   Click to choose a Caption Color.

3   Click to choose whether to make the caption opaque, translucent, semitransparent, or transparent.

4   Click to choose a Caption Style for your font, such as serif, sans-serif, or small caps.

5   Click to choose a size for your caption.

6   Click to choose a Caption Effect such as a drop shadow or raised text.

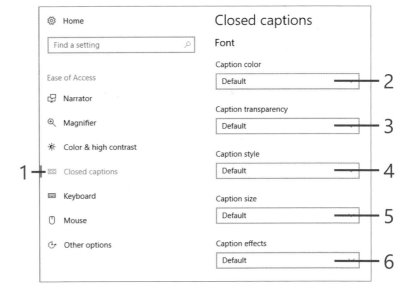

> **TIP**   You can see a preview of your choices in the Preview section of the Closed Captions settings. Some settings might make your captions harder to read against busy backgrounds, so you'll need to experiment.

# Using Speech Recognition

Have you ever imagined spraining your wrist and not being able to use a keyboard to enter text in apps on your computer? Speech Recognition is a feature built into Windows that you can use to provide speech input to your computer when you're using an application such as a word processor and then let your computer carry out entering the text you've spoken. When you activate Speech Recognition, you need to ensure that your microphone is set up and that the app begins to learn your spoken patterns. When you've performed this basic setup procedure, you can then use this app to provide input to your computer.

## Set up Speech Recognition

1  In the Cortana search box, type **windows speech recognition**.

2  In the results, click the Windows Speech Recognition Desktop App.

*(continued on next page)*

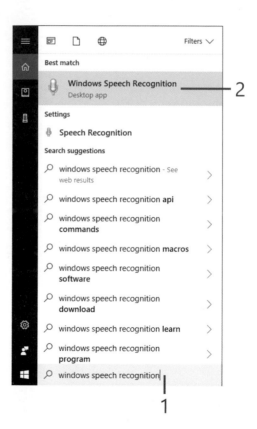

## Set up Speech Recognition  *continued*

**3**  Click Next.

**4**  Choose the type of microphone that you will use.

**5**  Click Next to proceed through several more screens of the wizard to make choices.

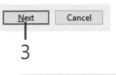

3

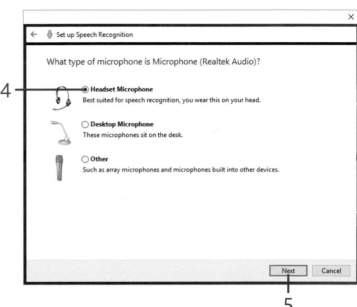

4

5

⚠ **CAUTION**   Speech recognition technology has come a long way since it was created, but it is still an evolving technology. When you dictate something using this feature, be sure to proofread it for any errors, which can range from your computer entering "to" when you meant "two," or missing a word in a sentence.

✓ **TIP**   After you set up Speech Recognition, you can type the phrase **speech recognition** in the Cortana search box and then press Enter. Speech Recognition opens in Listening mode. Speak a command such as "Open Excel," or, if you have displayed a document, you can speak words, numbers, or punctuation that you want to enter. To close the feature, click the Close button (X) on the Speech Recognition controls that appear near the top of the screen, or click the – symbol to minimize it.

# Using visual alternatives for sounds

Windows uses sounds to notify you of different events such as critical battery alerts or calendar reminders. If sound feedback when you're interacting with Windows is difficult for you to hear, you might prefer visual indicators. You can choose to have Windows 10 flash the active title bar, active window, or the entire display in place of sounds.

## Set up visual notifications for sounds

1   In the Ease of Access settings window, in the left pane, click Other Options.

2   Click the Visual Notifications for Sound drop-down list.

3   Click one of the three notifications options in the list to turn one on.

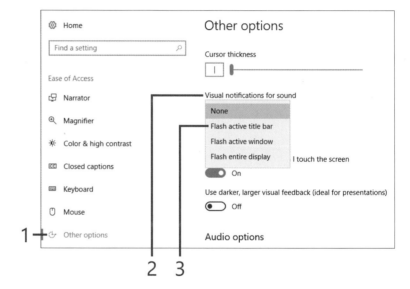

> ✓ **TIP**   To turn off visual notifications, in the drop-down list shown here, choose the selection None.

# Accessing and managing networks

# 8

A computer network makes it possible for several computers to join and share resources such as an Internet connection or printer as well as documents. Using Windows 10, you can create a new network, join an existing network (including public networks such as those in restaurants and airports), and make settings for sharing. Your home network or a public network you access from a laptop or tablet computer as you travel around functions using a technology called *Wi-Fi*.

Beyond knowing how to join and access a network, it's important to be aware of security and privacy settings so that those outside the network can't access your content and settings information.

# Understanding Wi-Fi networks

Wireless networks are everywhere. They provide an access point for computers to go online. Individuals need to connect to a network and provide a password. Networks can be public or private. Typically, a private network is secure, and, as such, only those who have joined the network can connect to it. You can find a public network in places such as a hotel, café, or library. These networks are open to anybody who gets the password from the network owner; they are, therefore, less secure.

### Understand how a Wi-Fi network works

A simple home network requires a piece of equipment called a *modem* connected to an incoming Internet connection through your provider (for instance, the cable or phone company). This modem is connected by a cable to a *wireless router*. Computers and other devices such as phones and tablets can use the wireless signal from the wireless router to access the

Internet connection and share resources. (Most Internet service providers offer an *Internet gateway* device that combines the functions of a modem and router into a single unit.)

You can connect each computer in your residence to your home network to share files, music, photos, and the like between devices. If there are peripherals such as a printer connected to the network, these also can be shared. Windows' *homegroup* function makes setting up file and device sharing a little easier.

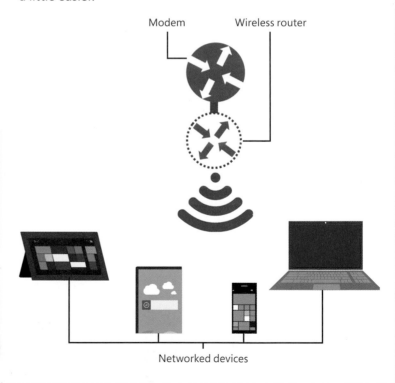

Modem      Wireless router

Networked devices

> **TIP** If you want to connect a single computer to the Internet, you can connect it directly to your modem (using an Ethernet cable) without going through a separate router. With this type of single PC setup, there's no need to broadcast the connection wirelessly to other computers (unless you want to use your single computer in multiple locations throughout your house), so no wireless router is required.

> **TIP** Virtually all computers today are Wi-Fi capable; however, if you have an older model that does not have Wi-Fi capability, you can buy a Wi-Fi adapter that plugs into a USB port on your computer. You can also purchase a *Mi-Fi* (mobile wireless) hotspot with which you can connect your computer to your cellular connection.

# Turning Wi-Fi on and off

Before you can connect to a home Wi-Fi network or a public Wi-Fi hotspot, you need to enable the Wi-Fi adapter built in to or connected to your computer. If you want to make your computer invisible to all Wi-Fi networks, you want to disable your Wi-Fi adapter.

## Enable and disable Wi-Fi

**1** On the taskbar, click the Network button.

**2** If your computer's Wi-Fi is enabled, the Wi-Fi button shows in color. Click the Wi-Fi button to disable the Wi-Fi adapter so you can't connect to Wi-Fi networks.

**3** To enable the Wi-Fi adapter, click the Wi-Fi button again.

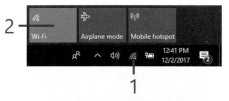

# Connecting and disconnecting

To connect to a Wi-Fi network, either at home or at a public Wi-Fi hotspot, you need to be within range of the network; depending on the network strength, this could be up to approximately 300 feet. Once you're in range, you can select the network you want and then provide a password, if required. After you join a network for the first time, many networks allow you to sign in at any time without providing the password each time.

## Connect to a network

1 On the taskbar, click the Network button.

2 From the list of available networks, select a network. The panel for the selected item expands.

3 If you want to connect to this network every time you log in to Windows 10, select the Connect Automatically check box.

4 Click the Connect button.

5 If you're connected to a secured network, enter the network security key (password) for that network.

6 Click the Next button.

7 If you're on a secured (private) network, click Yes to make your PC discoverable. If you're on a public network, click No.

> ✓ **TIP** Secured or private networks, like the one in your home, appear with a normal Wi-Fi icon in the network panel. Unsecured or public networks appear with a warning icon in addition to the Wi-Fi icon. Unsecured networks, such as those for public Wi-Fi hotspots, are not protected by encryption and are more easily hacked than secured networks. You should avoid accessing sensitive information, such as your online bank account, via unsecured networks.

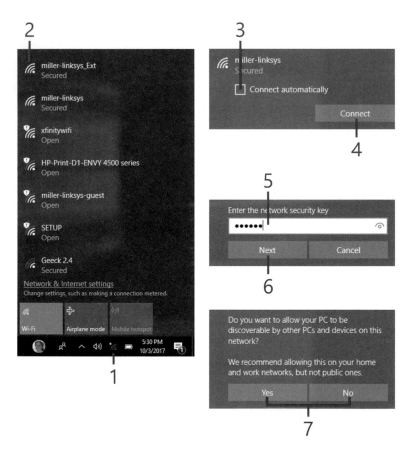

## Disconnect from a network

**1** On the taskbar, click the Network button.

**2** In the network panel, click Disconnect for the network to which you're connected.

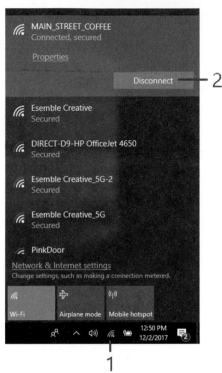

✓
**TIP** To get help with network problems, on the taskbar, right-click the Network button and then, on the shortcut menu that opens, choose Troubleshoot Problems. In the wizard that opens, make your choices and proceed through the wizard pages to see if Windows can detect and solve network problems.

✓
**TIP** When you're connected to a public network, your computer and the information it contains are always at risk. If you join a public network, it's a good idea to disconnect from it when you're done using it.

# Joining a homegroup

On a home network, you can set up a homegroup to make it easier to share items across the network. Any computer that belongs to the homegroup can easily share documents, printers, music, and videos with other computers and devices. You can control what you share with others (see "Setting file and printer sharing options" later in this section) via Windows Settings. Joining a homegroup requires that you get the homegroup password from the main computer in the homegroup; note that this is a different password from the one you use to connect to a network.

## Join a homegroup on a home network

**1** In the Settings window, click Network & Internet

**2** Click Status on the left side of the window.

**3** In the Change Your Network Settings section, click HomeGroup

**4** Click the Join Now button, and then, in the following screen, click Next.

*(continued on next page)*

1 — Network & Internet
Wi-Fi, airplane mode, VPN

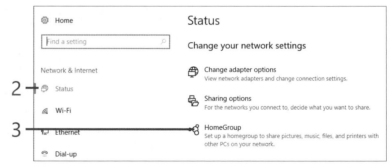

⊙ Home

[Find a setting]

Network & Internet

2 — ⊕ Status

⌁ Wi-Fi

⌁ Ethernet

☎ Dial-up

Status

Change your network settings

Change adapter options
View network adapters and change connection settings.

Sharing options
For the networks you connect to, decide what you want to share.

3 — HomeGroup
Set up a homegroup to share pictures, music, files, and printers with other PCs on your network.

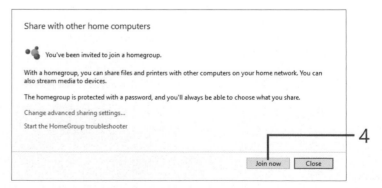

Share with other home computers

You've been invited to join a homegroup.

With a homegroup, you can share files and printers with other computers on your home network. You can also stream media to devices.

The homegroup is protected with a password, and you'll always be able to choose what you share.

Change advanced sharing settings...

Start the HomeGroup troubleshooter

4

[Join now]  [Close]

## Join a homegroup on a home network *continued*

**5** Click an item to make it Shared or Not Shared.

**6** Click Next.

**7** Type your homegroup password.

**8** Click Next.

**9** Click Finish.

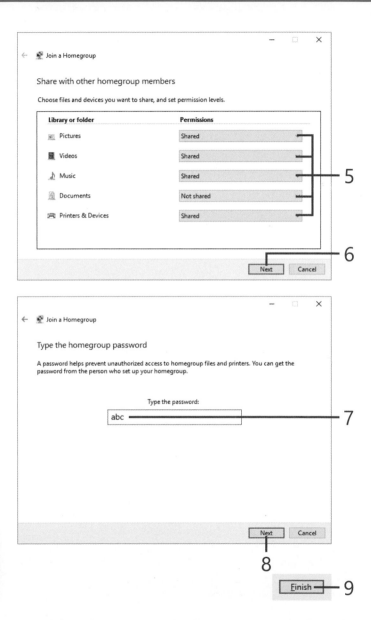

# Setting file and printer sharing options

Most people find that sharing files and a printer with others on a network makes life easier. You don't need to send files by email or share them online, and you don't need to have every computer on a home network physically connected to a printer. To turn on this functionality, you first need to configure File and Printer Sharing settings.

## Configure Sharing settings

**1** In the Network & Internet settings window, click Wi-Fi.

**2** In the Related Settings section, click Change Advanced Sharing Options.

**3** In the Private section, click Turn On File and Printer Sharing, if it's not already selected.

**4** Click Save Changes.

# Using Airplane Mode

When you're flying on an airplane, the flight crew usually requests that you turn off electronic equipment during takeoff or landing. With Windows 10, you can comply with this request while still being able to safely use your computer in flight by using Airplane Mode. Airplane Mode suspends all signal transmissions from Wi-Fi, Bluetooth, or a cellular connection so that they don't interfere with the plane's communications.

## Turn on Airplane Mode

**1** On the taskbar, click the Network button.

**2** Click Airplane Mode.

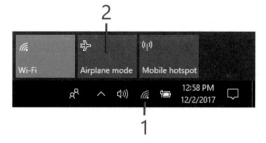

---

 **TIP** To turn off Airplane Mode, click the button in the Action Center again.

⚠ **CAUTION** With Airplane Mode turned on, you won't be able to send or receive email, or text or place calls using an Internet service such as Skype. As soon as you land and turn off Airplane Mode, however, you can retrieve any messages that have been sent while you were cruising the skies.

# Making your computer discoverable to Bluetooth devices

Bluetooth is a short-range wireless connection through which various devices can connect with one another. You might have paired your smartphone with your car or your computer to a printer via Bluetooth, for example. If you want your computer to be available for pairing with Bluetooth devices, such as a wireless mouse or keyboard, you need to make it *discoverable* by other devices.

## Make your computer discoverable

1 In the Settings window, click Devices.

2 Click Bluetooth & Other Devices.

3 If the switch for the Bluetooth is set to off, click to turn it on.

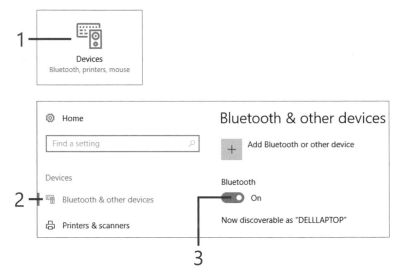

---

**TIP** This task makes your computer discoverable to other Bluetooth devices. You can also manually add a Bluetooth device to the computer by going to the Devices settings page and clicking Add Bluetooth or Other Device.

# Going online with Microsoft Edge

# 9

Microsoft Edge is the new web browser that comes with Windows 10. Edge sports a cleaner, simpler interface than most other browsers, which helps users concentrate on content rather than toolbars and menus. Within this interface, you can browse websites and search for content on webpages.

In addition to its simple interface, Edge offers features to keep you secure when browsing, and to keep track of favorite websites and your browsing history. Using Reading View, you can display articles without the clutter of ads and unrelated pictures that appear on many webpages. Also, you can draw on webpages and share them with others.

**In this section:**

- Getting an overview of Edge
- Setting a home page
- Browsing among webpages
- Viewing your browsing history
- Working with tabs
- Marking up webpages
- Using Reading View
- Adding items to Favorites or Reading List
- Using InPrivate browsing
- Finding content on pages
- Zooming in and out
- Managing downloads

## Getting an overview of Edge

Edge brings with it a new look and feel for a browser. To keep the interface clear from clutter, tools such as Favorites, Reading List, and History are accessed by using the Hub button. You can display a set of tools for marking up and sharing webpages by clicking the Make a Web Note button. Nesting these tools keeps the Edge toolbar uncluttered.

In addition to the simpler look, you can use the Web Note feature to draw on a webpage, insert typed comments, or highlight items, and then share that marked-up page with others. Edge is also the browser used by the Windows 10 personal assistant, Cortana, making it possible for you to perform advanced web searches from your desktop.

Toolbar          Tabs

Reading View     Hub      Share

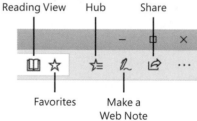

Favorites     Make a
Web Note

> **TIP** Because Edge is a newer browser than Internet Explorer or Google Chrome, some older webpages might not be compatible with it. In these cases, the page will open in the Internet Explorer browser instead.

# Setting a home page

When you open any browser, a home page appears. You can select the home page that Edge opens when you start it or click the Home button; in a sense, the home page acts as your home base for browsing the web. Perhaps you want a home page that displays current stock values or the weather, for example. You can set up more than one home page, and each will appear on its own tab.

## Specify a home page

1  Open Edge and then, in the top-right corner of the window, click the Settings and More button.

2  Scroll down the menu and click Settings.

3  Click the Open Microsoft Edge With pull-down menu.

4  Click to select A Specific Page or Pages.

5  In the Enter a URL box, type the address that you want to use as your home page.

6  Click the Save icon.

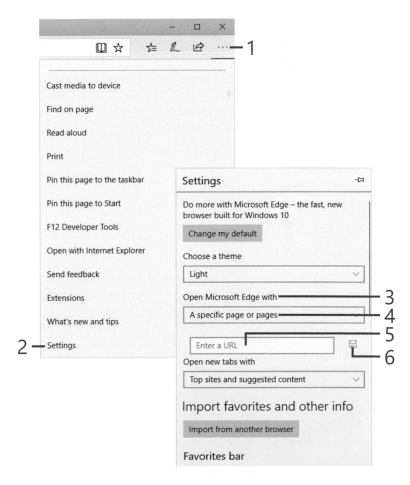

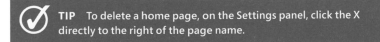

**TIP** To delete a home page, on the Settings panel, click the X directly to the right of the page name.

# Browsing among webpages

The main function of a browser is, as the name implies, to browse the Internet, going from website to website or from one page in a website to another. Each location on the web is uniquely identified by a URL, such as *www.Microsoft.com*. With Edge, you can use URLs to go to a particular site. You can also use the Back and Forward buttons to move back and forth between pages or sites that you've just displayed in your current browsing session.

## Move among webpages and sites

**1** With Edge open, in the Address bar, type a URL for a website. As you type, Edge displays suggested websites in a drop-down list.

**2** Press Enter to go to this address or select the site you want from the resulting drop-down list.

**3** Click the Back button to go to the previous page.

**4** Click the Refresh button to reload the page.

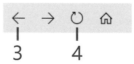

# Viewing your browsing history

When you use a browser, you leave a trail of sites that you've visited. It's often handy to be able to look at that trail to find a site you want to revisit when you've forgotten its URL. Using the History tab, you can look at your browsing history and click a site to go there again.

## See recently visited sites

**1** With Edge open, click the Hub button.

**2** Click the History tab.

**3** Scroll down to view the sites you've visited.

**4** Click to collapse the Last Hour setting and choose another timeframe for your history display.

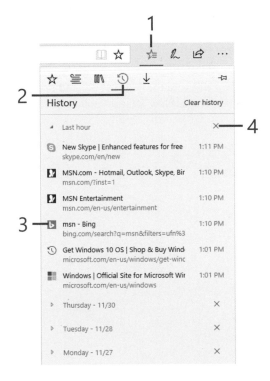

---

**TIP** To remove your history of sites visited—perhaps to keep your activities private from others—on the History tab of the Hub, click Clear History.

# Working with tabs

By using tabs in browsers, you can have several sites open at one time and move among them by simply clicking a tab. For example, if you were researching a topic, the ability to move among tabs to crosscheck facts would be very useful. You can also keep a tab open so that you can quickly return to it after some time spent dealing with another task and set aside groups of tabs for working on multiple webpages.

## Open a new tab

**1** With Edge open, click the New Tab button.

**2** Click a suggested site or type a URL into the Address bar and press Enter. After you go to a site, the words New Tab are replaced by the site name.

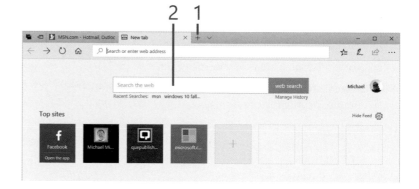

**TIP** To locate the URL of a site you've visited recently you can use the History feature, which was covered in the previous task.

## Manage tab groups

1 Open the tabs you want to set aside for future use.

2 Click the Set These Tabs Aside button.

3 To view a tab group you've saved, click the Tabs You've Set Aside button.

4 Click a thumbnail to reopen that tab.

5 Click Restore Tabs to add the saved tabs to your current browser view.

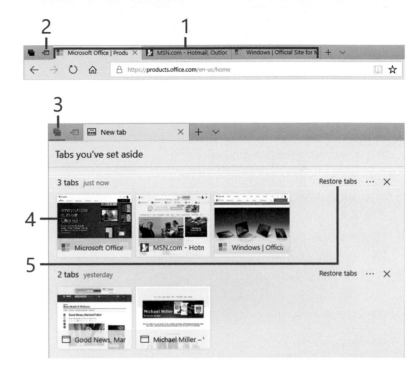

## Marking up webpages

Edge includes a new feature called Web Note. Using Web Note, you can turn on an editing mode in which you can write, draw, or insert typed comments on a webpage, and then share that markup with others or keep a record for yourself.

### Draw on webpages

1 With a webpage open in Edge, click the Make A Web Note button. This opens the Web Note toolbar.

2 Click the Pen tool and then draw on the page.

3 Click the Highlighter tool and then highlight some content on the page.

4 Click the Add a Note button and then, in the box that appears, type a note.

5 Click the Share Web Note button.

6 Click to select a person or app you want to share with, then enter the requested information to share the marked-up page.

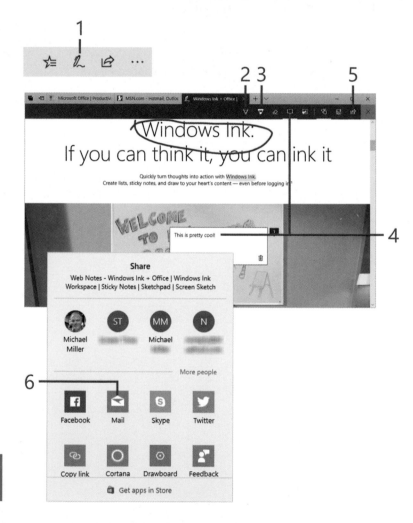

TIP   You can also use the Share button outside of the Web Note editing mode to share any webpage you like.

# Using Reading View

With Reading View, you can remove the clutter of a webpage to present the content in a more magazine-like style. Reading View enlarges the text of an article slightly, as well, making it easier to read. You open Reading View by clicking the Reading View button, which is located on the Address bar. However, be aware that Reading View works only with websites that support this feature.

## Open Reading View

**1** With an article open on a webpage in Edge, click the Reading View button.

**2** Click the Reading View button again to leave Reading View.

# Adding items to Favorites or Reading List

As you browse the Internet, you might find articles or information that you want to read but can't take the time to read them right at that moment. In that case, you can save them to your Reading List and come back to read them later. Likewise, you can save your favorite webpages in a Favorites list; just click a Favorite link and you're taken back to that page.

## Work with Favorites and Reading List

**1** With a webpage open in Edge, click the Add to Favorites or Reading List button.

**2** Click either Favorites or Reading List.

**3** Accept the default name or type a new name for the item.

**4** Click Add.

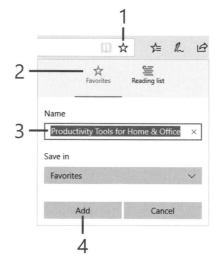

**TIP** For even faster access to your favorite pages, display the Favorites Bar at the top of the browser window, beneath the Address Bar. To do this, click the Settings and More button and select Settings to display the Settings panel, and then click the Show the Favorites Bar switch.

**TIP** If you choose to add an item to Favorites, you can also choose to create the item in Favorites or the Favorites Bar, or even create a new folder in which to save the item. After you click the Add to Favorites or Reading List button, click the Save In drop-down list and select a location.

# Using InPrivate browsing

When you browse the Internet, you can leave your browsing history open to others' eyes or allow sites to place tracking cookies on your computer that identify you to others. InPrivate browsing is a feature with which you can browse in privacy, thereby keeping your online actions secure.

## Keeping browsing data private

1 With Edge open, click the Settings and More button.

2 Click New InPrivate Window.

3 Type a URL and then press Enter to go to a website with InPrivate browsing active.

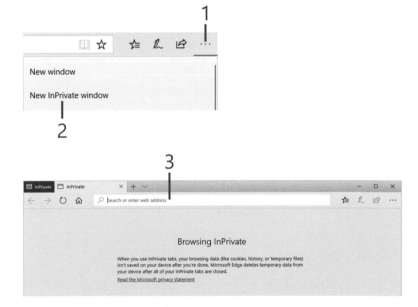

⚠ **CAUTION** InPrivate browsing opens a browser window that uses the feature; other browser windows do not, so be sure to use an InPrivate tab for any browsing that you want to remain private.

# Finding content on pages

A web browser is all about finding the information you need while you're online. Just as you might need to search to find content in a document, so might you also need to search for content on a webpage.

## Search for content on a webpage

1 With Edge open, click the Settings and More button.

2 Click Find on Page.

3 In the Find on Page box, type your search text.

4 Click the Forward button to view the next result.

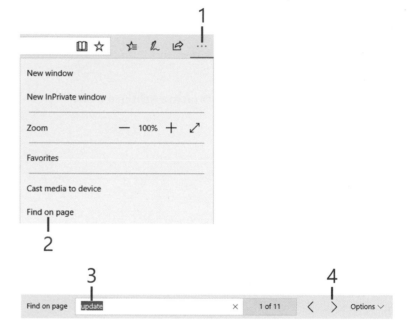

---

**TIP** To further refine your search, click Options, and then select Match Whole Word or Match Case.

# Zooming in and out

One of the benefits of reading content online rather than in a book or magazine is that you can adjust the size of that content easily. You can zoom in to view larger text and pictures, or zoom out to fit more on your computer's screen—whatever accommodates your reading preference.

## Enlarge or reduce a webpage

1 With a webpage open in Edge, click the Settings and More button.

2 To enlarge the view, in the Zoom control, click the Zoom In button.

3 Reduce the view, click the Zoom Out button.

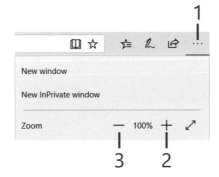

> ✓ **TIP** If you have a touchscreen computer, you can use your fingers to zoom in and out on a page. To zoom in, pinch your fingers together, place them on the screen, and then spread them apart. To zoom out, touch the screen with your fingers spread apart and then bring them together.

# Managing downloads

Often while you're browsing online, you will come across items that you want to download, such as an app, a piece of music, or an image. When you do this, in most cases your content is downloaded to the Downloads folder on your computer, though you can choose to download it to other locations. Your download history is available to help you keep track of this content.

## Manage your downloads

**1**  With Edge open, click the Hub button.

**2**  Click the Downloads tab. You now see files you've recently downloaded.

**3**  Click Open Folder to open the Downloads folder on your computer.

---

✓ **TIP**  To clear your download history, in the Downloads panel, click Clear All. To pin a downloaded item to the Start menu, click the Pin button.

---

✓ **TIP**  You can enhance Microsoft Edge with various *extensions* that provide added functionality to the browser. Click the Settings and More button, and then click Extension. You'll see any extensions you've previously installed; click Get Extensions from the Store to view and download additional extensions from the online Microsoft Store.

---

# Connecting
# with others

# 10

Even in this high-tech age, it's still true that our human contacts are often what matter most. In many cases, technology makes it possible for us to communicate with one another so that we can work on projects, share information, or connect with family or friends.

Windows 10 makes it easy to organize all the people you communicate with via the People app. Also, Windows provides sharing features through which you can share a photo or document via email or social-networking services such as Twitter and Facebook. And, new to the Fall Creators Update, you can now use your Windows 10 PC to send and receive text messages to and from your friends with mobile phones.

## In this section:

- Adding contacts in People
- Editing contacts
- Linking contacts
- Sharing contacts
- Using My People
- Sending and receiving text messages

# Adding contacts in People

From new friends to new business acquaintances to new favorite restaurants, we gain more contacts all the time. The Windows People app is a great centralized place to keep that information. You can copy contacts from your Microsoft email accounts to save you time, and add copies, one by one, from within the People app itself. If you include an address for a contact, a link is added that you can use to display that address in the Maps app.

## Add a contact

**1** Click the Start button.

**2** Click the People app tile or item in the All Apps list.

*(continued on next page)*

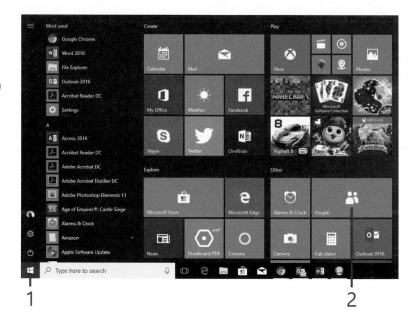

## Add a contact *continued*

**3** Click the Add button.

**4** Click a text box to add information such as Name, Mobile Phone, or Personal Email.

**5** Click Save.

**TRY THIS** All of your contacts are listed in the left pane of the People app. Click any contact name to view full details for that contact.

## Editing contacts

Things change, and so do your contacts' phone numbers, email addresses, and even names. Editing the information for a contact is a simple matter of opening the contact's record, making any changes to the information it contains, and then saving the record.

### Edit a contact

**1** With the People app displayed, click a contact.

**2** Click the Edit button.

**3** Click a text box and add information or edit existing information.

**4** Click Save.

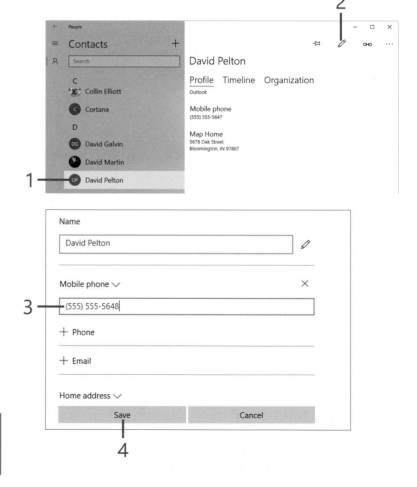

# Linking contacts

If you add contacts from multiple sources, you may end up with two or more contacts for the same person. The People app enables you to link two or more contacts together so that all the information for that person or entity exists under a single record.

You can also use this feature to link a colleague and his or her assistant's contact information, for example, or link the records for your grandchildren so that you can find them in one spot.

## Link contacts

1 With the People app open, click a contact.

2 Click the Link button.

3 Click the Choose a Contact to Combine button.

4 Click the contact you want to link.

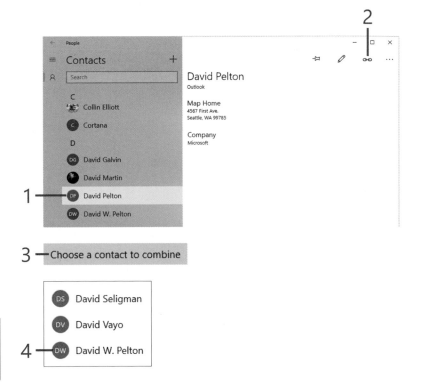

---

TIP To edit a linked contact, select the contact you used to establish the link. Click the Edit button, and then click the linked contact's name. The record for that contact then opens for editing.

---

TIP To remove the link, in the Contacts list, click the contact you used to establish the link, and then click the Link button. Click a contact listed there, and then click Remove.

---

## Sharing contacts

People often want to share contact information with friends or coworkers. In the People app, you can share contact information easily. The methods available to you depend on what apps (such as Twitter or Mail) you have installed and set up.

### Share a contact

**1** With the People app open, in the left panel, click a contact.

**2** In the right panel, click the See More button.

**3** Click Share Contact.

**4** Click Confirm

*(continued on next page)*

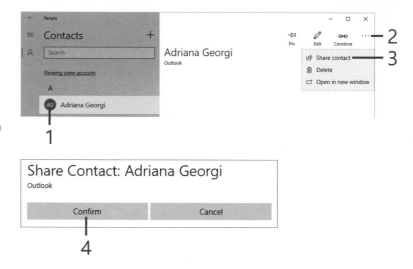

## Share a contact  *continued*

**5**  Click a Share option such as Mail or Skype.

**6**  If sending via Mail, provide an addressee and any other information.

**7**  Click Send.

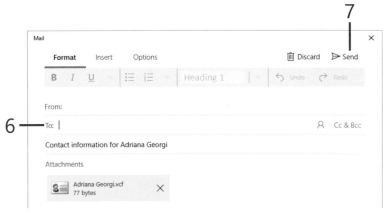

# Using My People

You don't have to open the People app to manage and message your contacts. Windows 10's My People function, new in the Fall Creators Update, lets you add icons for your favorite contacts to the Windows taskbar; you can then message those people directly from the taskbar.

## Add a contact to the taskbar

**1** Click the People icon in the taskbar's notification area to open the My People pane.

**2** Click the People tab to view suggested favorites.

**3** Click the Apps tab to open the People, Mail, or Skype apps.

**4** Click Find and Pin Contacts to display all your contacts

**5** Click the contact you want to add to your taskbar.

 **TIP** You can add contacts from your People app, or those stored in the Mail and Skype apps.

## Send email and other messages from My People

1 Click a person's icon on the taskbar to view the My People pane for that individual.

2 Click the back arrow.

3 Click People to view that person's contact and other information.

4 Click Mail to send that person an email.

5 Click Skype to initiate a Skype conversation with that person.

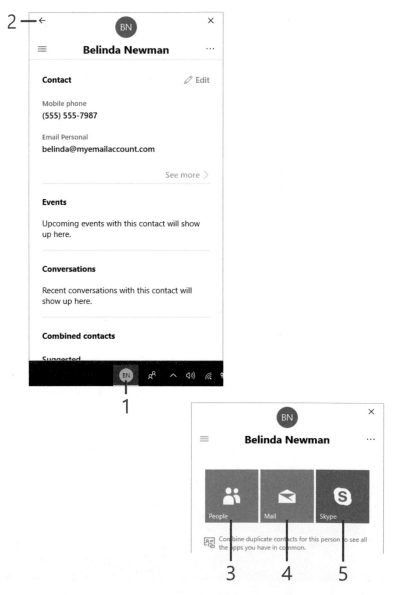

**TIP** When you click Mail, you then need to click the New Mail (+) icon to complete and send an email message.

**TIP** When you click Skype, you can opt to send a text message or initiate a video or audio call.

# Sending and receiving text messages

You use your phone to send and receive SMS text messages. Windows 10 now lets you link your computer to your phone, so you can send and receive text messages on your PC. This functionality uses Cortana, Windows 10's virtual personal assistant.

## Receive a text

1 If you see an alert notification for a text, type your reply into the Reply box.

2 Click the Send arrow.

3 To view other texts, click the Action Center icon on the taskbar.

4 Recently received texts are displayed here in the Action Center. Enter a reply to a text within the Reply box.

5 Click the Send arrow to send the text.

> **TIP** Before you send and receive text messages on your PC, you must link your computer to your mobile phone. You'll need to install the Cortana app on your smartphone (see your phone's app store) and sign into your Windows account from the Cortana app. Messages sent to your phone will now also be displayed on your Windows 10 computer.

## Send a text

1 Click within the Cortana search box in the taskbar and enter text [name], and then press Enter. (Replace [name] with the name of someone in your contacts list. For example, to text Sherry, enter **text sherry**.)

2 Enter the text of your message.

3 Click Send.

# Using Mail

# 11

Email was one of the first forms of online communication, long before
tweets and texting, and it's still very much in use today. In a business
setting, email is still the go-to form of communication because it accommodates longer messages with larger attachments, and you can document
those communications in a permanent way.

With the Mail app in Windows 10, you can set up email accounts you've
created in services such as Outlook and Gmail and access all your messages
in one central location. Using the Mail app, you can receive, respond to, and
forward email messages, and download email attachments. You can also
use email folders to organize the messages you receive.

## In this section:

- Setting up email accounts
- Reading email messages
- Opening an attachment
- Replying to a message
- Forwarding a message
- Creating a new message
- Formatting message text
- Adding attachments
- Moving emails to folders
- Deleting emails

# Setting up email accounts

Before you can use an email account in Mail, you must set it up. The account actually exists in an email service such as Outlook or Yahoo! By setting it up in Mail, you can access that account from the Mail app. You can set up multiple email accounts and switch among them easily. This makes it possible for you to have a central access point for your work email account and one or more personal accounts.

By default, the Mail app is configured to use the email account associated with your Windows account. You can at any time, however, add other email accounts to the Mail app, and work with multiple accounts.

## Set up a new email account

1  Open the Mail app and click the Settings button.

2  Click Manage Accounts.

3  Click Add Account.

*(continued on next page)*

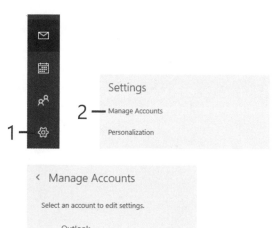

## Set up a new email account *continued*

**4** Click the type of account that you want to set up.

**5** Type your email address and click Next.

**6** Type your password and click Sign In.

**7** You might be asked to give permissions depending on the type of account you chose in step 4. When your account is set up, click the Done button.

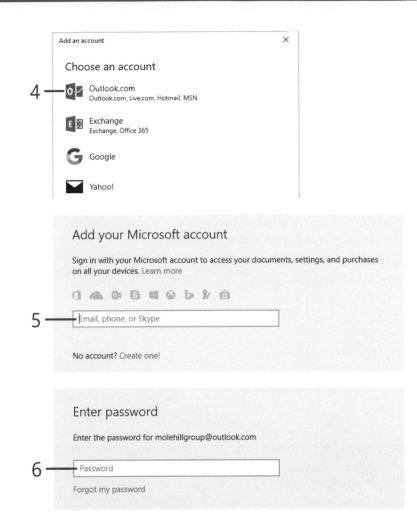

> ⊕  **TRY THIS**   To switch to another account within the Mail app, click the All Accounts button on the left and then click the name of the other account. You now switch to that account's inbox.

# Reading email messages

Email is all about exchanging text messages and sometimes sharing attached documents. After you set up one or more mail accounts in Mail, when you click the Mail tile, you are taken to the Inbox of the last active account. From the Inbox, you can scroll to locate a message and then open and read it.

## Open and read an email message

1 With an email account open in Mail, click the message you want to read.

2 The selected message opens. To delete this message after you've read it, click the Delete button. (If you don't see the Delete button on the toolbar, click the Actions button first.)

3 Click the Back button to return to the Inbox.

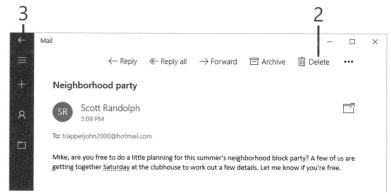

> **TIP** Email messages in the Mail app are organized by the date received, with today's messages at the top. The Inbox item in the left pane indicates how many emails are contained in your Inbox.

> **TIP** To make email messages easier to read, expand or maximize the Mail window. When the window is large enough, you see three distinct panes—from left to right, the Navigation, Messages, and Contents panes.

# Opening an attachment

Some email messages that you receive contain attachments. These are files carried with the email that you can open and view or save. Attachments come in a variety of formats, based on the application in which they were saved. (It's common, for example, to send pictures as attachments.)

## Work with attachments

1 With the Mail app open and an Inbox selected, click a message with an attachment. (If a message has an attachment, you'll see a paper-clip icon as part of the message header.)

2 Click the attachment to open it. (If the attachment is a picture file, a thumbnail of that picture may appear within the message.)

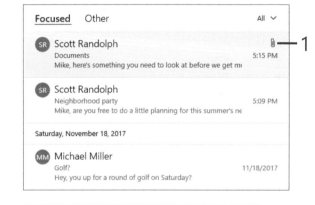

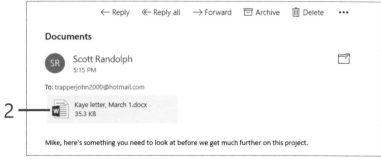

**TIP** In step 2, you can also right-click the attachment and choose either Open or Save. Clicking Save opens File Explorer, which you can use to locate a folder where you can save the file.

# Replying to a message

When you read an email, you might want to reply to the sender or to the sender and all other recipients of the original message. When you open a message and choose a reply command, the message displays a new message area above the original contents. You then type your reply and send it.

## Reply to email

1 With the Mail app open, click an email message to display it.

2 Click the Reply or Reply All button.

3 Type a message.

4 Click Send.

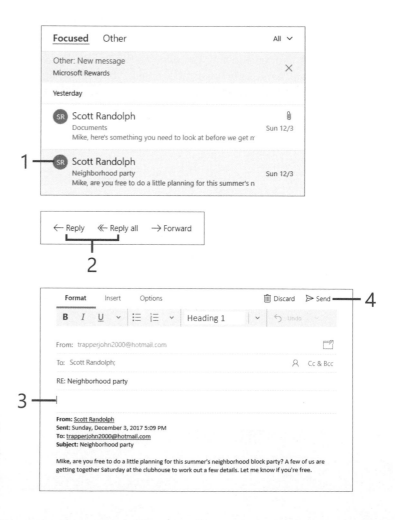

> **TIP** The choice between replying to just the sender or replying to the sender and all recipients (Reply All) is typically based on whether you want to share your response with all recipients or only the original sender. For example, if you receive an email from someone organizing a meeting and you want to let him know you'll be five minutes late, does everybody else really need to receive and read your email?

# Forwarding a message

Some messages are worth sharing. When you receive a message, in addition to replying to it, you can forward it to others. Any attachments to the original message will be forwarded, as well.

## Forward a message

1 With the Mail app open and an email message displayed, click Forward.

2 In the To box, type one or more email addresses.

3 Type a message.

4 Click Send.

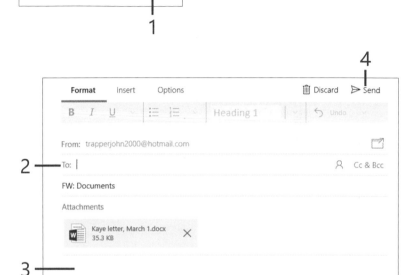

> **CAUTION** When you forward a message without the sender's permission, use your judgment about whether what you're sharing would be appropriate. If you think the sender has shared confidences or content with you that she would prefer remain private between you, forwarding the message or attachments might violate the sender's trust.

# Creating a new message

Though you'll spend much of your time reading and replying to emails, you'll also spend time creating your own messages. You can send emails to a single recipient or to a group of recipients. You can also copy people you consider tangential to the discussion, but whom you want to keep informed. Finally, you can *blind carbon copy* (BCC) those whom you want to keep in the loop but without other recipients being aware of them.

## Create an email message

1 With the Mail app open, in the left panel, click the New Mail button.

2 Click the To box, and then type one or more addresses.

3 Click the Cc & Bcc link, if required, to open boxes in which you can add copy and blind-copy recipients addresses.

4 Click the Subject box, and then type a subject for the message.

5 Click within the message area and type your message.

6 Click Send.

> **TIP** If you change your mind about sending the message, you can cancel it by clicking the Discard button, located near the top-right corner, to the left of the Send button.

> **TRY THIS** When creating a message, you can set its importance, language, and run a spelling check by clicking the Options button. Click the Importance, Language, and Spelling buttons to toggle between low and high importance, choose a language from a drop-down list, or run a spelling check before sending the message.

# Formatting message text

You have probably used the tools in a word-processing app to format text in documents, applying styles such as bold or italic, bullet or numbered lists, or setting font styles. Mail offers many of these same basic formatting tools, and you can use them to emphasize or organize text in your emails.

## Format a message

**1** With a new message open, make sure the Format tab is selected. (If not, click Format at the top of the message.)

**2** Select the text you want to format and then click the Bold, Italic, or Underline button.

**3** To format an entire paragraph, click within that paragraph, click the Styles drop-down list, and then select a style such as Emphasis.

**4** To create a bullet list, select one or more lines of text, click the Bullets button, and then select a list style from the drop-down list.

**5** Click Send to send the formatted email.

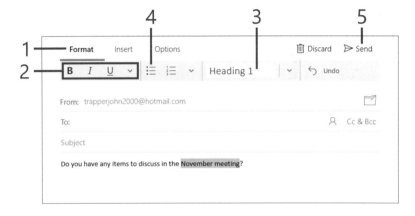

 **TIP** You can click the arrow between the List and Styles options to display additional paragraph formatting. These options include indenting settings, text alignment and spacing settings, and spacing before and after paragraphs.

**TIP** After you apply formatting, if you decide that you don't like the effect, use the Undo button to remove the formatting.

# Adding attachments

Being able to attach documents of all kinds to emails gives you the ability you to communicate lengthier content quickly. Your attachments can be in any file format, though it might require that the recipient have the originating application on his computer to open it.

## Attach a file

1 With a new email created in the Mail app, click the Insert tab.

2 Click Add Files.

3 Browse to locate the file that you want to attach.

4 Click Open.

5 The file is added to your message. Type any accompanying text as necessary.

6 Click Send.

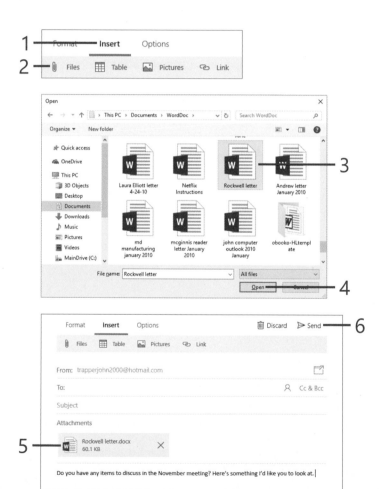

> **TIP** When attaching a picture file, use the method described here (with the Add Files button) to attach the file to your email message. Only use the Pictures button if you want to insert the picture within the body of the email message.

# Moving emails to folders

You can organize the Inbox in your originating email account (such as Outlook or Gmail) into folders, and those folders will be available in the Mail app. In Mail, even though you can't create new folders, you can move emails that you receive in Mail into the existing folders from your email account. This helps you to keep a record of messages in an organized way.

## Move email to a folder

1 With a message open in Mail, toward the top-right corner, click the Actions button.

2 Click Move.

3 Click a folder.

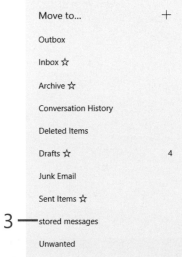

**TIP** To view all folders for an email account, click the All Folders button in the Navigation pane.

# Deleting emails

You probably don't want to save every email message you get. Instead, you might prefer to delete certain messages after you read them. Deleted messages are actually saved in a Deleted Items folder for a time, but as that folder fills, older messages are purged from it. You can delete an open email by clicking the Delete button. To delete messages from your Inbox, you can use two methods.

## Delete email

1   In the Messages pane of the Mail app, click the Enter Selection Mode button.

2   Select a check box to the left of a message.

3   Click the Delete button.

4   Move your mouse pointer over another message.

5   Click the Delete This Item button, located on the right side of the message itself.

> **TIP**   To delete multiple emails, use the Enter Selection Mode button in the Messages pane, and then select multiple check boxes before clicking the Delete Selected Item(s) button. To select all the messages in your inbox at once, click the check box above the list of messages.

# Shopping for apps in the Microsoft Store

# 12

The Microsoft Store is a handy way to download both free apps and those that you purchase, which you can then use on your Windows-based computer or tablet. You access the Microsoft Store with the Store app, which is included with Windows 10. The Microsoft Store also includes games (covered in Section 20, "Playing with Xbox games"), movies and TV shows (see Section 14, "Recording and watching videos"), and books.

In this section, the focus is on buying apps. Apps provide you with functionality ranging from entertainment to maps to drawing. You can also get productivity applications such as Microsoft Word, PowerPoint, or Excel in the Microsoft Store.

Whether you buy an app in the Microsoft Store or choose one that is free, it is downloaded to your computer over the Internet. The Store app also keeps your existing apps up to date by downloading the latest updates, either automatically or manually.

## In this section:

- Exploring the Microsoft Store
- Searching for apps
- Creating payment information for an account
- Updating Windows apps
- Reading reviews
- Buying an app
- Rating an app

# Exploring the Microsoft Store

The Apps section of the Microsoft Store includes a variety of collections and categories that help you browse for apps. For example, one of the first sections of the Apps page is a list of apps labeled Apps We Picked For You; this list is based on other purchases you've made. Beneath that are lists of Top Paid Apps and Top Free Apps, as well as New Apps, Best-Rated Apps, and so on, as you scroll down the page.

Using the two links on the left side of the page, you can explore apps on top-rated charts and apps currently featured in the Store. You can also scroll to the bottom of the Apps home page to browse apps by category, such as Food & Dining, Kids & Family, and News & Weather.

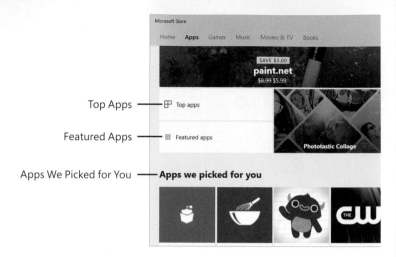

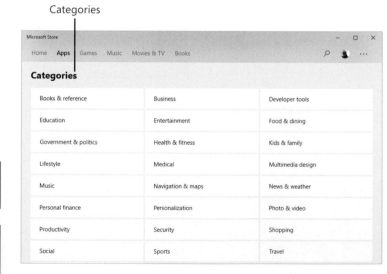

 **TIP** To see more apps in the lists that run across the Store screen, on the right side of the list, click the Show All link.

 **TIP** Don't confuse the online Microsoft Store, discussed here, with the physical Microsoft Stores that sell Windows-related computers and devices in malls and other locations across the country.

# Searching for apps

You can use the built-in search feature in the Store app to find apps either by providing the app name or a phrase about the type of app for which you're searching. A search will return results across all categories, not just the Apps section of the Store.

## Find an app

1 With the Microsoft Store open, click the Search (magnifying glass) icon. This opens the Search box

2 Type an app name or search term, such as **calculator**.

3 As you type, matching apps are listed. Click to select one of these apps or press Enter to complete your search.

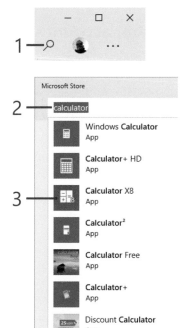

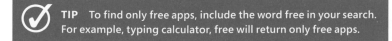

**TIP** To find only free apps, include the word free in your search. For example, typing calculator, free will return only free apps.

# Creating payment information for an account

When you set up Windows 10 initially, you provided information about your Microsoft account or created a new account. To make purchases from the Microsoft Store, you need to add payment information to that account. After you have done that, you can make purchases using that account.

## Add payment information to your account

1 From within the Store app, click the See More button.

2 Click Payment Options and then sign in to your Microsoft account if requested.

3 The Microsoft Account page opens in your web browser. Click Add a Payment Option.

4 Check the type of payment option you want to add: credit/debit card, bank account (for electronic withdrawal), or PayPal.

5 Click Next.

6 Enter payment and billing details, and then click Next to finalize the new payment method.

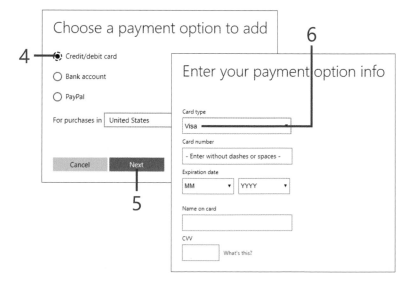

> **TIP**   Each user account that you use to log in to Windows can have separate Payment & Billing settings. You can, therefore, pay for purchases from, say, your child's account using a different payment option than the one you use for your home business account.

# Updating Windows apps

After you have purchased or downloaded a free app from the Microsoft Store, when an update to that app becomes available, you can download it from the Store. By default, updates are downloaded and installed automatically. If you'd rather download one or more updates manually, at this moment, you can do so.

## Manually update your apps

**1** From the Store app, click the See More button.

**2** Click Downloads and Updates.

**3** Recent updates are listed here. Click Get Updates to download and install any available updates for your apps.

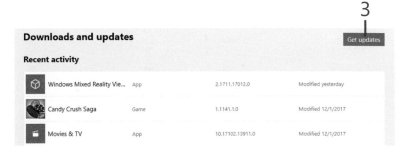

> ✓ **TIP** If you don't want to automatically download updates, click See More, and then click Settings. On the Settings page, click the Update Apps Automatically switch off.

# Reading reviews

Users of the Microsoft Store can rate the apps they obtain. Those ratings can help you and others make choices among apps. If you're not sure about whether to buy or download a free app, check out its reviews before you make your decision.

## Read others' reviews

**1** With the Microsoft Store open, click an app that you're considering buying.

**2** Scroll down to the Ratings and Reviews section. The bar chart shows ratings by number of stars, from 1 to 5.

**3** To be able to read all reviews, click Show All.

**4** Scroll down to read the individual reviews.

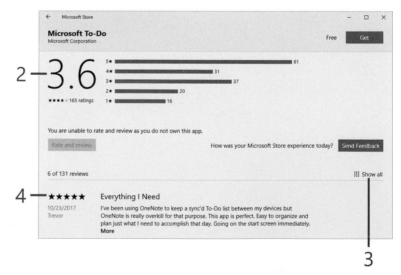

# Buying an app

When you have set up payment options for your account, you can easily buy apps or content in the Microsoft Store. Some apps are free, and some require that you purchase them; either way, obtaining and installing them works similarly.

## Buy an app

**1** In the Microsoft Store, click the app you'd like to download.

**2** If the app is free, click the Get button to download it to your computer.

**3** If it's a paid app, click the Buy button. When prompted, enter your Microsoft account password.

**4** Accept or change your purchase method.

**5** Click Buy.

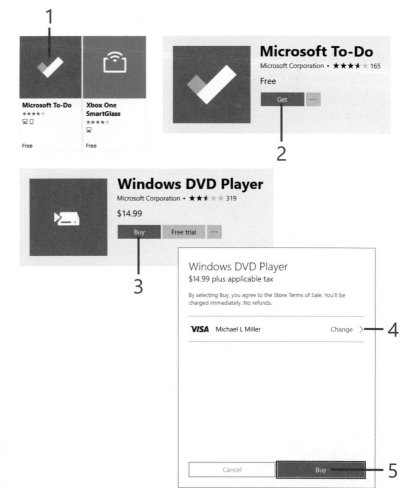

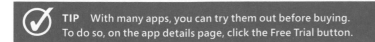

**TIP** With many apps, you can try them out before buying. To do so, on the app details page, click the Free Trial button.

# Rating an app

Just as reviews might have helped you find the right app for your need, your review of an app can help guide others. After you've used an app for a while, consider going back to the store to rate it.

## Rate an app

**1** Open the details page for an app you already have installed, and then scroll down to the Ratings and Reviews section.

**2** Click the Rate and Review button.

**3** Click the Rate This Item list and select a star to rate the app from 1 to 5 (1 being the lowest rating and 5 the highest).

**4** Type a headline for your review into the Give It a Headline box.

**5** Type your review into the Tell Us What You Like and Don't Like box.

**6** Click Submit.

1

**Ratings and reviews** | Most recent ∨ | PC ∨

4.4

5★ ▬▬▬▬▬▬▬▬▬▬▬ 1,122
4★ ▬▬▬▬▬▬ 457
3★ ▬▬ 76
2★ ▪ 20
★★★★★ 1,766 ratings   1★ ▬ 91

Rate and review          How was your Microsoft Store experience today?   Send Feedback

2

☀ MSN Weather

Rate this item                    Select a platform

3 ──  Choose a star rating    ∨      PC    ∨

Write a review

Give it a headline

4 ──  [                              ]

Tell us what you like and don't like

5 ──  [                              ]
      [                              ]

0/1,000

Will post publicly as Michael
Microsoft may email you a response from the developer, but won't share your email address. You can opt out of future responses by using the link in the

6 ──  [  Submit  ]          [  Cancel  ]

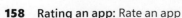

**TIP** If you don't want to post your own comments about an app, consider rating the reviews that other people have written as helpful or not helpful. In the Ratings and Reviews section of an app's details page, click Yes or No under a review to endorse it or suggest it wasn't that helpful to you.

# Enjoying music

# 13

For many people, listening to music on a computer has replaced using a fancy stereo system or radio. Computers make it possible for you to assemble a virtual music library taken from DVDs or downloaded from online sites. You can use your computer's speakers to deliver your music and use your computer controls to adjust volume and speaker settings.

The Groove Music app in Windows 10 is your tool for organizing and playing the music you have stored on your computer.

## In this section:

- Adding music files to the Groove Music app
- Playing music
- Adjusting volume
- Creating playlists

# Adding local music files to Groove Music

You use the Groove Music app to play music you've previously downloaded or ripped to your computer. To do so, you need to tell the app where you've stored your music.

## Choose where Groove Music checks for music files

1 With the Music app open, click the Settings button.

2 Click Choose Where We Look for Music.

3 By default, the app looks for music in the Music folder. To add another location, click the Add button.

4 Locate and select the folder that contains the music you want.

5 Click the Add This Folder to Music button.

6 Click Done.

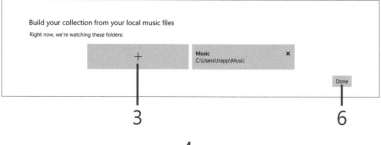

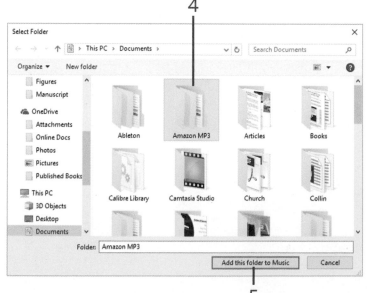

> **TIP** You can also listen to music over the Internet via streaming music services, such as Spotify (www.spotify.com) and Pandora (www.pandora.com). Use your web browser to go to these websites or download a service's app (if available) from the Microsoft Store.

# Playing music

The main function of the Groove Music app is to play music. You first locate the track or album that you want to play, and then you use the playback controls to play, pause, or move forward or backward one track at a time.

## Play a song

1   With the Groove Music app open, click My Music.

2   To view and play individual songs, click the Songs tab.

3   To view and play all music by a given artist, click the Artists tab.

4   To view and play specific albums, click the Albums tab.

5   To play a complete album, or all songs by a given artist, click Play All.

6   To play an individual song, click the track name, and then click the Play button for that track.

7   Click the Pause button to stop playback.

8   If you're playing an album, click the Back button to move to a different track. If you're playing an individual song, clicking this button brings you to the beginning of the song.

9   If you want the track to repeat when it ends, click the Repeat button.

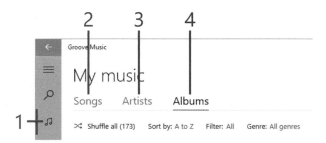

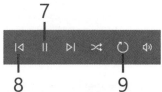

**TIP**   To shuffle music in your library so that songs play in a random order, click the Shuffle button in the playback controls (it looks like two crossed arrows).

# Adjusting volume

There are two volume settings that you can control: the system volume for your Windows 10 computer, and the playback volume in an app (such as the Groove Music app). The system volume sets the overall level of volume for your device, and an app volume is set relative to that.

## Adjust Music or system volume

**1** With the Groove Music app open and music playing, in the app's playback controls, click the Volume button.

**2** Drag the Volume slider to adjust the volume.

**3** On the taskbar, click the Speakers/Headphones button.

**4** Drag the volume slider to adjust volume.

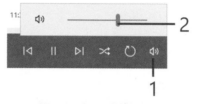

> ✓ **TIP**    To fine-tune your speaker and system sound volume, right-click the Speakers/Headphones button, and then, from the shortcut menu that opens, choose Open Volume Mixer. You can then adjust the speaker volume and system sound volume (for example, for notifications of new emails) separately.

> ✓ **TIP**    To mute the sound from within the Groove Music app, click the Volume button, and then click the Mute button (which looks like a small Volume button) next to the slider. Click the Mute button again to unmute the sound.

# Creating playlists

You use the Groove Music app's playlists feature to assemble your own virtual albums from more than one source. You might create one playlist of dance music, another for a kids' birthday party, and still another for a romantic evening at home. You can create as many playlists as you like from the music you have available in the Groove Music app.

## Create a new playlist

**1** With the Music app open, click Create New Playlist.

**2** Click Name This Playlist and type a name for the playlist.

**3** Click the Create Playlist button.

*(continued on next page)*

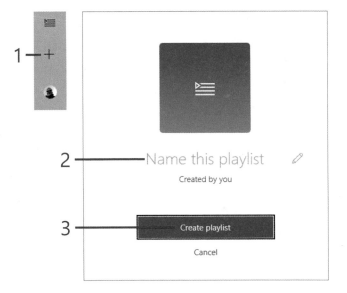

(continued on next page)

**TIP** To play a playlist, click Playlists in the navigation sidebar to view all your playlists. Mouse over the playlist you want to hear, and then click that playlist's Play button.

## Create a new playlist *continued*

**4** The new playlist appears on the right side of the app; it's currently empty. Click Go to Albums.

**5** Navigate to and select a song you want to add, and then click Add To for that song. (Alternatively, click Add To at the top of the album page to add all tracks from this album to the playlist.

**6** Click the name of the playlist. The song is now added to that playlist; repeat steps 5 and 6 to add more songs to the playlist.

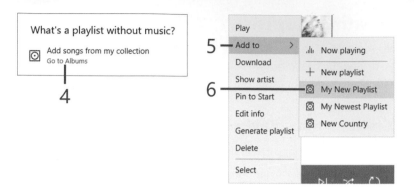

What's a playlist without music?

⊙ Add songs from my collection
   Go to Albums

4

5 — Add to

6 —

| Play | |
|---|---|
| Add to > | ⅲ Now playing |
| Download | + New playlist |
| Show artist | ⊙ My New Playlist |
| Pin to Start | ⊙ My Newest Playlist |
| Edit info | ⊙ New Country |
| Generate playlist | |
| Delete | |
| Select | |

✓ **TIP** To place a playlist on the Start menu so that you can quickly play it, open the Playlists screen, right-click the playlist, and click Pin to Start. To unpin it, go back to the playlist screen and click Unpin from Start.

# Recording and watching videos

# 14

Today, computers are used as much to play video as they are to create word-processed reports. With Windows 10, you can use the Camera app to capture your own videos and the Movies & TV app to buy programs and play them back.

In this section, you make use of all three apps to create or locate content and use playback controls to watch videos. You also use the Microsoft Store to buy or rent video content and open a world of available programs.

## In this section:

- Recording your own videos with the Camera app
- Buying videos
- Locating videos in the Movies & TV app
- Playing videos
- Configuring settings in the Movies & TV app

# Recording your own videos using the Camera app

All notebook computers (and many desktops, too) are equipped with a camera with which you can capture still photos or create video recordings. With Windows 10, you use the Camera app to record video and then view the recorded video in either the Photos or Movies & TV app.

## Record a video

1 Open the Camera app and click the Video button to switch to video mode.

2 Click the Video button again to begin recording.

3 Click the Pause button to pause recording; click the button again to resume recording.

4 Click the Stop button to stop recording.

> **TIP** To use the Camera app to take selfie photos, click the Photo button to switch to Photo mode, and then click the Photo button again to take a picture.

# Buying videos

The online Microsoft Store offers a wide variety of movies and TV shows that you can rent or buy. First, you must have set up payment options for your Microsoft account (for instructions on how to do this, see the task "Creating payment information for an account" on page 154). After you're set up, you can use the Store app to purchase the programming you want. (When you purchase TV shows, you have the option of buying a season pass or individual episodes.)

## Shop for movies

1 Open the Store app and click Movies & TV.

2 Scroll down to browse for movies and TV shows.

3 Alternatively, click the Search box or button to search for a specific item.

4 Click the item you want to purchase.

5 Click the Buy button.

*(continued on next page)*

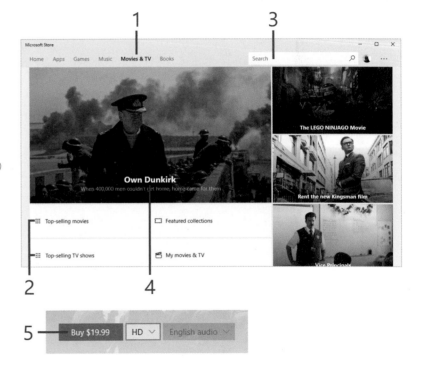

> **TIP** In step 5, for some items you can also click the Rent button. If you do, you'll be asked whether you want to stream or download the movie or show before proceeding with signing in to your account.

## Shop for movies *continued*

**6** Type your password.

**7** Click Sign In.

**8** Click Buy to purchase the item.

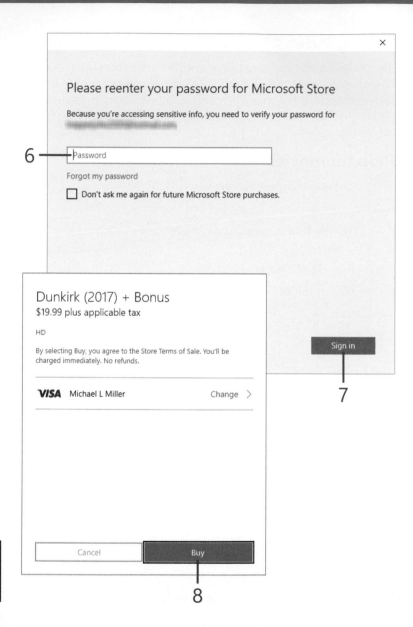

6 ———

7

8

> **→** **TRY THIS** When you open the detail window for a movie, you often find a button for watching a trailer. Click this to view the trailer for the movie before making your buying decision.

# Locating videos in the Movies & TV app

After you have created or purchased a number of videos, there are a few tools that you can use to locate those videos. The app divides videos by Purchased and Personal. You can also use the Search tool to locate videos by name, no matter what category in which they are saved.

## Browse for videos

**1** With the Movies & TV app open, click the Purchased tab to browse movies and TV shows you've previously purchased.

**2** Click the Personal tab to view all videos you've shot with the Camera app or downloaded from another video camera to your PC.

**3** Click a video to begin playback.

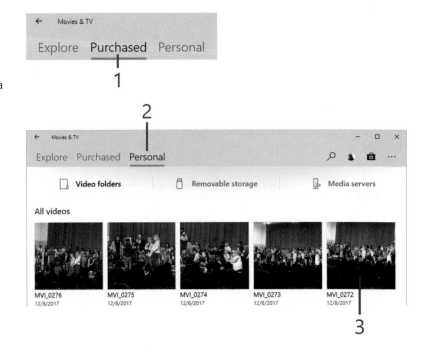

 **TIP** You can also search for videos by title. Click the Search button and then enter a full or partial name for the video you're looking for.

 **TIP** You can use the Sort By, Category, and Source fields at the top of the Purchased page to organize your videos.

# Playing videos

When you have recorded, downloaded, or rented a video, you can play it in the Movies & TV app. You can use the playback controls to pause, adjust the aspect ratio, adjust volume, turn on closed captioning for shows that support that feature, and expand the video image.

## Play a video

**1** With the Movies & TV app open, click the video you want to play.

**2** Click the Full-Screen button to make the video fit your entire computer screen.

**3** Click the playback slider to move forward or backward in the video.

**4** Click the Pause button to pause playback. Click the button again to resume playback.

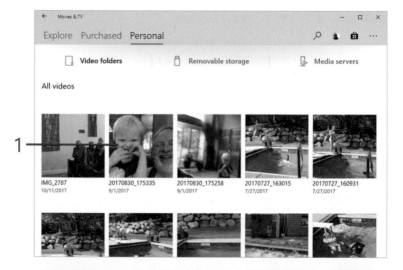

> ✓ **TIP**  You can use a playback tool named Cast to Device to cast the movie to a compatible device such as a smart TV. To cast a video to a smart TV, it must be on and have a Bluetooth connection. Click the More Options menu button, click Cast to Device, and then select a playback device from the list.

# Configuring settings in the Movies & TV app

You can play video at different quality settings, which can affect your viewing experience.

## Configure video settings

**1** From the main page of the Movies & TV app, click the More Options button.

**2** Click Settings.

**3** In the Download Quality section, click either the HD or SD option to choose that quality option as the default for future downloads.

**4** In the Playback section, click the switch on if you always want to start playback in full-screen mode.

**5** In the Mode section, click to select either Light or Dark mode for viewing (or accept the default to use whatever mode is selected for your entire system).

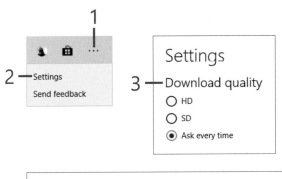

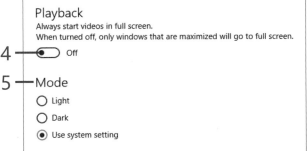

TIP   To make changes to your account billing or other information, use the links under the heading Accounts, on the right side of the Settings window.

# Working with the Camera and Photos apps

# 15

Though you might be used to taking photos with your smartphone, you might be unaware that your computer probably has a built-in camera. Using the Camera app that comes with Windows 10, you can take selfies or pictures of your surroundings. You can then use the Photos app to edit those photos in a variety of ways. Photos offers tools that you can use to enhance a photo, apply effects, adjust brightness, and crop or rotate it.

You can also create a slideshow from your photos and share them with others, or use the new Story Remix feature to create exciting video shows from your photos and videos. Of course, if you no longer need a photo, you can easily delete it.

## In this section:

- Taking photos with the Camera app
- Viewing photos in the Photos app
- Editing photos
- Enhancing photos
- Cropping photos
- Rotating photos
- Creating a slideshow
- Creating a Story Remix
- Setting a photo as your Lock screen or desktop background
- Sharing photos
- Deleting photos

# Taking photos with the Camera app

In a computer, the camera is typically placed above the monitor, whether you own a laptop or desktop model. When you turn on the Camera app, the camera takes pictures of whoever or whatever is facing the monitor. The main purpose of a computer camera is to capture video of the person using the computer for an online video call.

## Snap a photo

1  Click the Start button.

2  Click Camera.

3  Position your computer so that it's aimed at what you want to capture (so if you're taking a selfie, smile at the camera!), and then click the Take Photo button.

4  Click the Camera Roll button to open Photos with the photo displayed.

> ✓ **TIP**  Photos that you take with the Camera app are saved to the Camera Roll folder within the Pictures folder. The Photos app organizes photos into collections, such as those taken on a certain day, and albums that are created for you containing the best in a series of shots taken around the same time.

# Viewing photos in the Photos app

You view your photos in Windows 10's Photos app. The Photos app lets you view your photos in a number of ways. If you choose Collection on the Photos home page, you see every image you've taken organized by the month in which they were taken.

Also, you can create albums of photos, organized however you like. The Photos app also attempts to organize photos by the people in them and lets you view photos by the folders in which they're stored on your computer.

## Browse your photos

1 With the Photos app open, click Collection to view your photos by month taken.

2 Click Albums to view albums of photos you've created.

3 Click Create, and then click Album, to create a new album.

4 Click People to view photos organized by the main subject of each photo.

5 Click Folders to view photos as stored in their original folders.

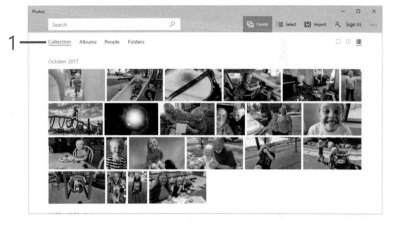

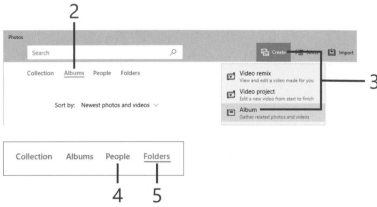

# Editing photos

We're not all professional photographers, and, unsurprisingly, our photos aren't always perfect. So, it's useful that you can edit a photo after you take it. The Photos app provides several useful tools for editing photos. For example, you can apply filters that change the hue of the picture, or you can modify the light to brighten an image or apply higher contrast.

## Use photo editing tools

1 Open the Photos app and then click a photo in a Collection to display it.

2 Click the screen to display the toolbar, and then click Edit & Create.

3 Click Edit.

4 Click the Enhance tab.

5 Click a filter to apply it.

6 Click the Adjust tab.

7 Click the and drag the slider on any control (Light, Color, Clarity, Vignette) to make that adjustment.

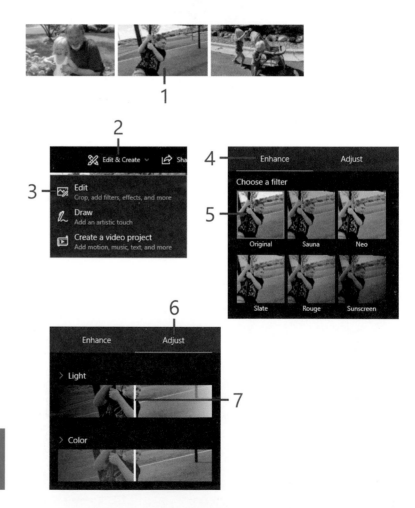

> **TIP** Click the right-arrow next to Light or Color to display more detailed editing controls, such as Contrast, Exposure, Tint, and Warmth.

# Enhancing photos

If you don't want to play around with applying different settings such as light and filters, you can use a single enhancement tool that applies multiple setting changes to produce what the Photos app considers to be the best photo possible.

## Enhance an image

1 With the Photos app open and the Edit tools displayed, click the Enhance tab if it's not already selected.

2 Click Enhance Your Photo. The automatic enhancement is applied.

3 Click and drag the slider in the Enhance Your Photo tile to apply more (right) or less (left) of the enhancement.

4 If you're not satisfied with the result, click the Undo All button to cancel the enhancements.

5 When you're satisfied, click the Save button.

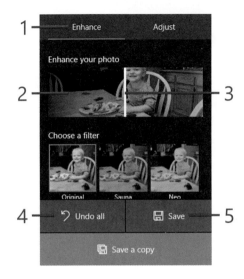

TIP If you want to keep a copy of your original photo before any enhancements or editing, click Save a Copy. This keeps a copy of the original and a copy of the enhanced version.

# Cropping photos

Just as not every photo we take comes out as bright as we'd like, some include people and things in the background we never intended to include. By cropping your photo, you can whittle away sections that you don't want, leaving just the portions of the image that you want to keep.

## Crop photos in the Photos app

1 With the Photo app open and the Edit tools displayed, click Crop & Rotate.

2 Drag any corner handle inward. When the image appears as you want, release your mouse button.

3 Click Done to confirm the changes.

1

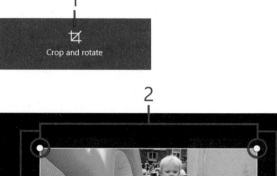

2

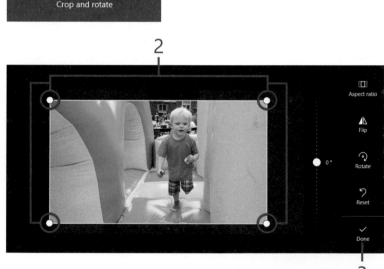

3

 **TIP** You can drag the handles on an image to be cropped inward, outward, to the right, left, up, or down.

**TIP** While using the Crop tool, you can click the Aspect Ratio button at the top of the screen to set parameters for the changes in your image's size. You can, for example, indicate you want the cropped image to be square, maintain the original aspect ratio, or display as widescreen.

# Rotating photos

Though you're not likely to hold your computer upside down and therefore capture an image upside down, you might want to rotate a photo to place it in a document at an angle as a special effect. The Photos app offers a Rotate tool with which you can pivot an image in 90-degree increments.

## Rotate a photo

1 With the editing tools displayed in the Photos app, click Crop & Rotate.

2 Click the Rotate button once to rotate the image 90 degrees clockwise.

3 Click the Rotate button again to continue rotating the image clockwise.

4 If you want to undo a rotation, click the Reset button.

5 Click Done to save your changes.

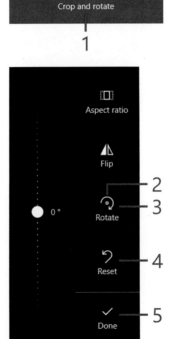

> **TIP** Rather than clicking the Undo button, another way to revert the image to its original orientation is to simply click the Rotate button until it's back to where it started.

# Creating a slideshow

One photo can show a moment in time, but several photos shown sequentially can tell a story. Using the Photos app, you can create a slideshow from a collection of photos. With the slideshow feature, you can display one photo after another and stop the slideshow at any time.

## Create and run a slideshow

**1** With the Photos app open on the home screen, click a photo in a collection to open it.

**2** Click the See More button to expand the menu.

**3** Click Slideshow to begin the slideshow.

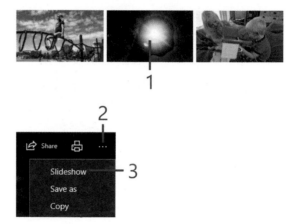

## Creating a Story Remix

You can use Windows 10's new Story Remix feature to create sophisticated video slideshows, complete with fancy transitions and background music. The easiest way to create a Story Remix is to have the Photos app do it for you, based on the photos you select—although you can also create Story Remixes with custom transitions, background music, and more.

### Create an automatic Story Remix

**1** From within the main page of Photos app, click Create.

**2** Click Video Remix.

**3** Click to select those photos and videos you wish to include in your Story Remix.

**4** Click the Add button.

**5** When prompted, enter a title for this project.

**6** Click Create Video.

**7** The Photos app creates the Story Remix and begins playback. Click Remix It for Me to randomly change the order of the photos in the Remix.

**8** Click Close when done.

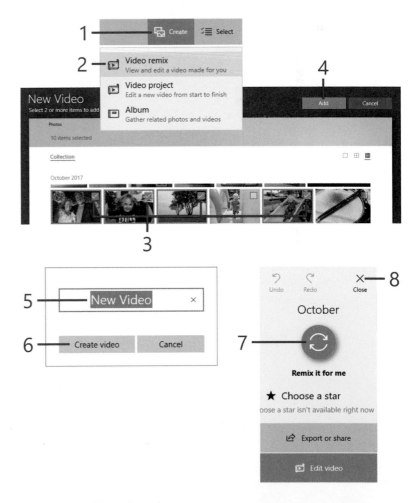

# Create a customized video project

**1** From the main page of the Photos app, click Create.

**2** Click Video Project.

**3** Click to select the photos and videos you want to include in this project.

**4** Click Add.

**5** When prompted, enter a title for this project.

**6** Click Create Video.

*(continued on next page)*

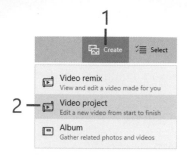

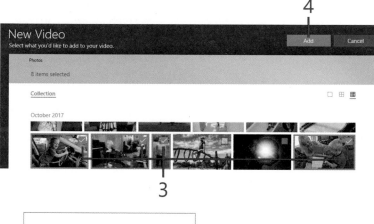

## Create a customized video project *continued*

**7** You now see the video editing screen, with your selected photos automatically added to the timeline at the bottom of the page. Click and drag any item to a new position, if you want.

**8** Click to edit an item on the timeline.

**9** Click Duration to change the length of time this item appears in the video.

**10** Click Filters to apply a photo filter to this item.

**11** Click Text to overlay words onto this item.

**12** Click Motion to choose how this item appears onscreen.

**13** Click Themes to apply a prepared visual theme to this project.

**14** Click Music to choose which background music plays for this video.

**15** Click the Play button to play this video.

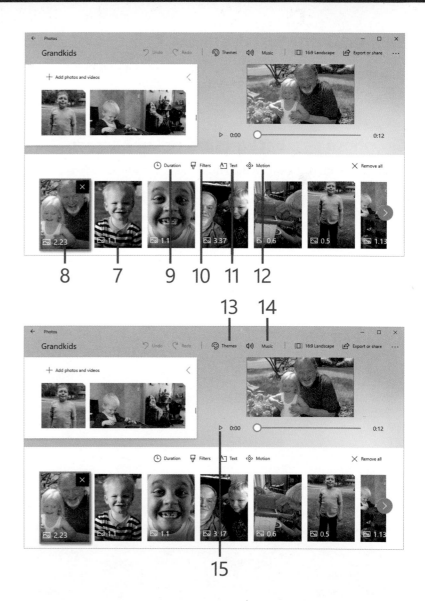

# Setting a photo as your Lock screen or desktop background

If you have a favorite photo, rather than frame it and put it on your desk, why not make it the image for your desktop or Lock screen background? With a photo displayed in the Photos app, you can set it up to be used as the background to either your desktop or the Lock screen that appears when your computer has gone to sleep.

## Set photo as a background or Lock screen

1  With a photo displayed in the Photos app, click the See More button.

2  Click Set As.

3  Click Set as Lock Screen (to set as your Windows Lock screen) or Set as Background (to set as your desktop background).

> **✓ TIP**  To stop using the photo as a background, right-click the desktop, and then, in the shortcut menu that opens, choose Personalization, and then choose a different background from Windows pictures, or choose a solid color.

# Sharing photos

When you take a great photo, it's hard to avoid the urge to share it with others. With the Photos app, you can share photos via Facebook, Twitter, the Mail app, and other apps and services.

After you set up the Mail app to use one or more email accounts, it's a simple procedure to send a photo by email. (See Section 11, "Using Mail," for more about how to do this.)

## Share a photo via email

1 With a photo displayed in the Photos app, click the Share button.

2 Click Mail. (If you have multiple email accounts, you'll now be prompted to select the account you want to use.)

3 Type an email address.

4 Type a subject.

5 Type a message.

6 Click Send.

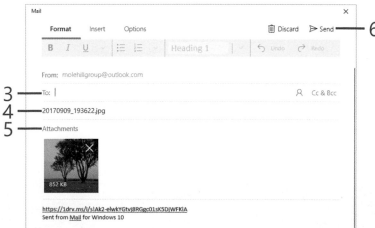

> ✓ **TIP** To share via Facebook or Twitter, you need to have those apps already installed and have accounts set up.

> ✓ **TIP** If you want to create a printed copy of a photo, display it in the Photos app, and then click the Print button. Use the Print pane that appears to print your photo.

# Deleting photos

If your Photo collections become crowded over time, making it difficult to find what you need, you might consider deleting some photos. You can delete a single photo or select several to delete in one action.

## Delete photos

1 With a photo collection displayed on the Photos home screen, select the check box for one or more photos you want to delete.

2 Click the Delete button.

3 In the confirmation prompt that appears, click Delete.

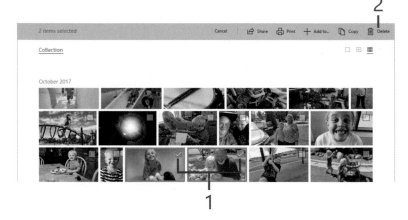

**CAUTION** Deleting a photo in the Photos app also deletes it in the Photos folder in File Explorer.

# Keeping on schedule with Calendar

# 16

Using the Calendar app included with Windows 10, you can view calendars, create events, and share those events with others via email. You can view calendars by day, week, or month. You can even view your work week only, leaving weekends out of the picture.

You can include special calendars such as a Birthday calendar or U.S. Holidays calendar in your display so that all events on these calendars appear in line with your own calendar events. The Birthday calendar will include birthdays of your Facebook friends.

## In this section:

- Displaying Calendar
- Changing views
- Adding an event
- Using Cortana to add an event
- Inviting people to an event
- Editing an event
- Changing work week settings
- Displaying U.S. Holidays and Birthday calendars
- Deleting an event

# Displaying Calendar

The Calendar app displays as a tile on the Start menu by default. When you open it, the current month appears in the top-left pane. You also see a pane that you can adjust to show a larger calendar by day, week, work week, or month. You can switch between months, both past and future, as well.

## Open the Calendar app

1 Click the Start button.

2 Click the Calendar tile.

3 Click the Forward or Back button to view the next or previous month.

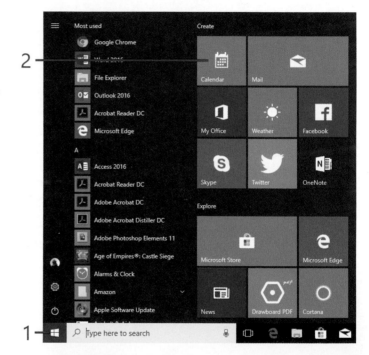

# Changing views

The Calendar app enables you to view your schedule by the day, week, or month. Also, you can view just those days during your work week, whether that week runs from Sunday through Thursday or Monday through Friday.

## View different time increments

1  With the Calendar app open, click the Day button to display today's calendar.

2  Click the Week button to display a weekly view.

3  If additional views are not displayed, click the Show button.

4  Click Month to display a monthly calendar.

5  Click Year to display a yearly calendar

6  To display a view of your work week, mouse over the Week button, click the down arrow, and then click Work Week.

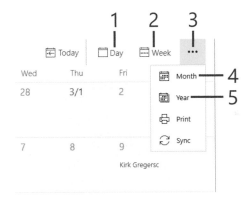

# Adding an event

The entire point of a calendar app is to give you the means to schedule various events, from a luncheon to a business meeting, and have the app remind you of an upcoming occasion.

With the Calendar app, you can create an event and specify the time and length for that event as well as a location. You can even choose which calendar to display it on, such as My Calendar or the Birthday calendar.

## Create a new event

1 With the Calendar app open, click New Event.

2 Type an Event Name.

3 Click the Location box, and then type a location.

4 In the Start Date and End Date boxes, click the calendar icon and set the dates.

5 In the Start Time and End Time boxes, click the drop-down arrows and set a time for each.

6 Click Save and Close.

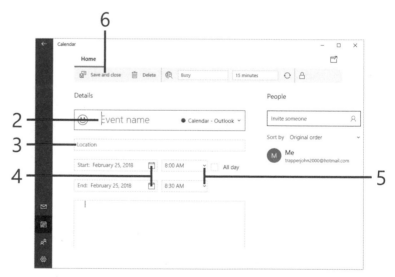

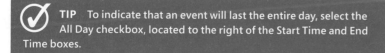

**TIP** To indicate that an event will last the entire day, select the All Day checkbox, located to the right of the Start Time and End Time boxes.

# Using Cortana to add an event

Cortana is your personal assistant, and as such, she can search the Internet, open apps, and even set appointments for you.

## Ask Cortana to create an event

1 Click the microphone button in the Cortana search box and ask Cortana to add an event to your calendar.

2 Follow the prompts to add details for the event.

By speaking your appointment details to Cortana rather than typing them, you have a hands-free way to add events to your calendar.

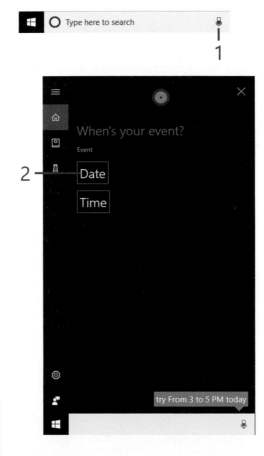

✓ **TIP** To add a reminder, click the Notebook button (second button from the top on the left side of the Cortana window), and then click Reminders. The reminders that you create here are displayed in the Notifications area of the Action Center.

# Inviting people to an event

When you create an event such as a meeting or party, you can use the Calendar app to include other people in the event. By inviting others, you notify them of the event details and give them a way to convey their intentions by replying Yes, No, or Maybe.

## Invite others to an event

1   From within the Calendar app, create a new event and enter details such as name, location, start, and finish times.

2   In the People section, click within the Invite Someone box and start typing the name or email address of the person you want to invite.

3   As you type, the Calendar app displays a list of people who match your query. Click the name of the person you want to invite.

4   Enter more people to invite, if you want, and then click Send.

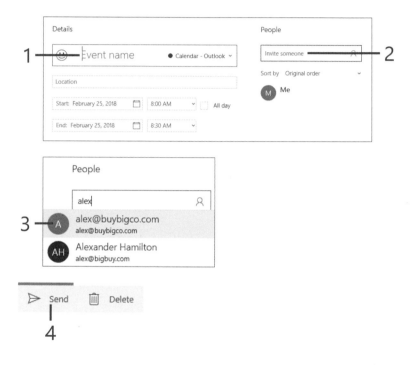

# Editing an event

Sometimes your plans change. When you want to edit an event to change the date, time, or invitees, you can do so easily and even inform everyone of the changes at the same time.

## Edit event details

**1** With the Calendar app open, click an event.

**2** This opens the event for editing. Make changes to any field.

**3** To remove an invitee, right-click that person's name and then click Remove.

**4** Click Save and Close (if there are no invitees) or Send Update (if there are others invited to this event).

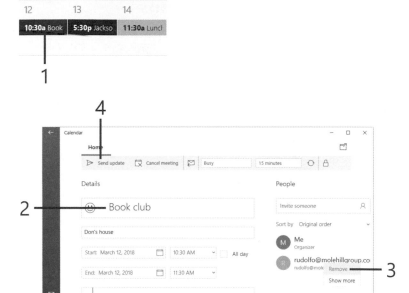

> **TIP** If you have invited people to the event and you make changes to it, clicking the Send Update button informs those people of your changes.

# Changing work week settings

If you use your computer for work-related activities, you might want to designate the days that make up your work week. For example, if you work Monday through Friday and click the Work Week view, you will no longer see Saturday or Sunday displayed. If you choose Thursday through Sunday, you have a four-day work week. You can also set working hours.

## Choose your work week

1 With the Calendar app open, click the Settings button.

2 Click Calendar Settings.

3 Click the First Day of Week box, and then choose the starting day of your week. A check mark is placed in that day's check box.

4 Click the check box for the last day of your work week.

5 Scroll to the Working Hours section and click the Start Time and End Time boxes and choose relevant times.

6 Click back in the Calendar to close the Calendar Settings pane and save your changes.

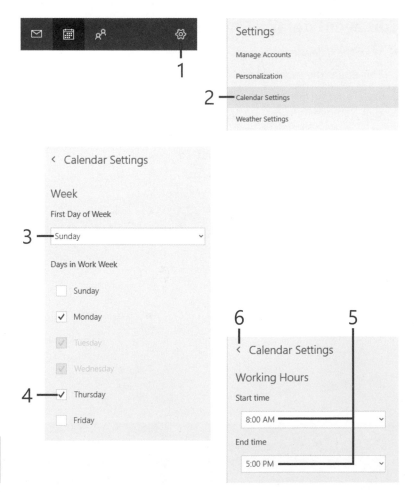

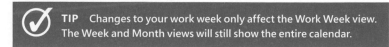

**TIP** Changes to your work week only affect the Work Week view. The Week and Month views will still show the entire calendar.

# Displaying the Holidays and Special calendars

Your email account might contain certain secondary calendars whose contents you can display on your calendar. For example, Outlook calendars can include United States holidays and birthdays. And, birthdays can be placed on your calendar by social networking sites such as Facebook.

## Add special calendars

1 With the Calendar app open, scroll through the list beneath the calendar in the left pane and check those special calendars you want to display. Uncheck those you don't want to see.

2 Click Add Calendars.

3 Select a type of calendar from the list on the left.

4 Click the calendar you want to add on the right.

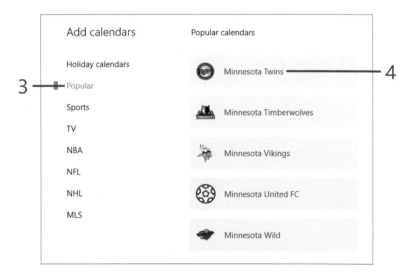

TIP To redisplay any unchecked calendars in the Calendar app, just click it again. When a calendar check box is filled with a color (rather than white), it's currently displayed.

# Deleting an event

Our schedules change in spite of our best efforts to organize ourselves. Sometimes, it can be something as simple as an appointment being canceled. Deleting an event from the Calendar app is simple and helps you avoid getting a notification about an event that's no longer going to happen.

## Remove an event from your calendar

1   Click an event to open its Details page.

2   Click Delete.

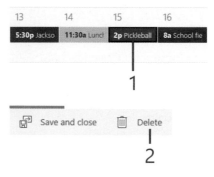

# Tracking your news, sports, and stocks

# 17

Windows 10 includes several preinstalled apps such as News, Sports, and Money. Each app boasts some robust features, so the purpose of this section is to introduce you to some of the more interesting ones. Feel free to explore each app on your own to discover even more functionality.

## In this section:

- Reading news articles
- Adding and turning off interests
- Choosing a sports category
- Adding a Sports favorite
- Creating an investment Watchlist
- Viewing markets

# Reading news articles

You can use the News app included with Windows 10 to keep you up to speed on current news stories. You can view the news articles in various categories such as U.S., World, Crime, and

Technology. You can also permit MSN News to access your location so that you can receive local news.

## Read the news

1 Open the News app and click one of the news categories at the top of the screen.

2 Click a news story to read it.

3 Scroll down to read more of the article.

4 Click the Forward button to view the next story.

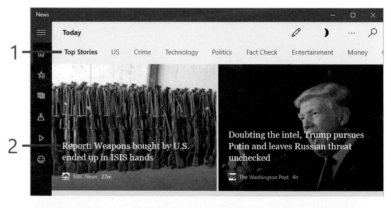

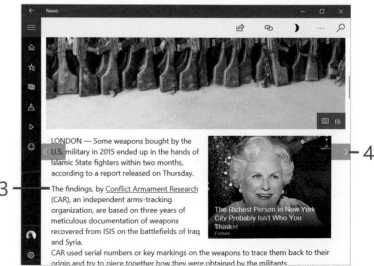

> **TIP** If your interests tend toward video news, click the Videos button in the navigation pane. The News app will display videos related to current news items. You can also use the Search box in the News app to search for stories related to a word or phrase.

# Adding and turning off interests

Not everyone shares the same interests, so the News app gives you the option to pick and choose what topics to include in your news. For example, you might leave out World news and include only U.S. news, or add interests such as animals or religion.

## Add or turn off a topic of interest

**1** With the News app open, click the Interests button.

**2** The My Interests category is selected by default, with your current categories displayed. Click the green star icon for a topic to remove it from your news feed.

**3** Click All Interests.

*(continued on next page)*

## Add or turn off a topic of interest *continued*

**4** Click a category to add it to your news feed. (The star icon turns green.)

**5** Alternatively, type a term into the search box.

**6** In the suggested results, click an item to select it, and then click the desired category to add it to your feed.

5

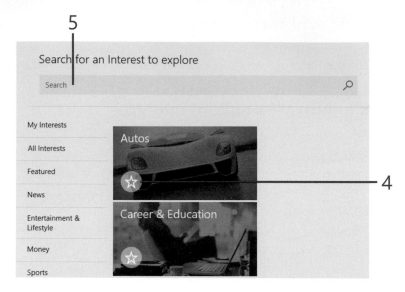

4

6

> **TIP** If you have a category of interest that doesn't fit within the broad category of interests that the News app provides, use the Search box to type a term related to that interest, such as Broadway, and then click the Search button to view matches.

# Choosing a sports category

Most sports addicts have their favorite games, teams, and athletes. Some might like football, baseball, and basketball, but how many also like hockey, golf, soccer, and tennis? If this description fits you, you'll enjoy the Sports app and how you can choose the sports news that you want to review.

## Display a sports category

1 Open the Sports app to display current sports news. Click a tile to read the entire article.

2 In the navigation pane, click a button to display articles within a sports category such as Golf or Major League Soccer.

3 Along the top of the screen, click to display Results, Schedule, Standings, Leading Players, and more for the selected sport.

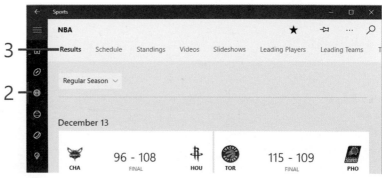

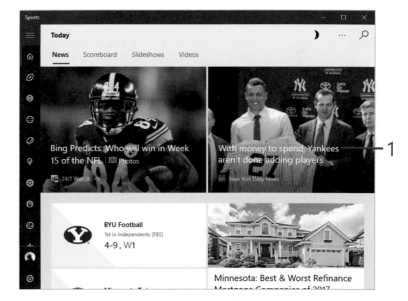

**TIP** There are quite a few sports categories. To make a particular category easier to find, in the top-left corner, click the Menu button to expand the navigation pane to include category titles.

## Adding a sports favorite

Just as you can customize many apps to display your favorite activities or categories, you can customize the Sports app to add favorites. Using the Favorites feature, you can follow a particular sport or team, saving you time as you peruse all the sports and scores that are out there.

### Add a favorite sport or team

1 With the Sports app open, scroll down the navigation pane and click the My Favorites button.

2 Your current favorites are now displayed. Click a team or sport tile to view more information.

3 To add a new favorite team, click the Add button.

4 Type a team name.

5 Click a team name in the search results to add that team as a favorite.

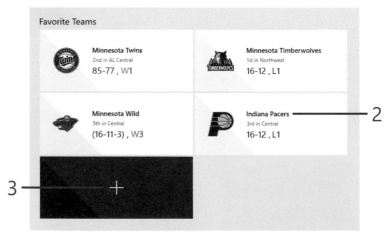

> **TIP** To view the latest scores when you're on the Sports home screen, near the top-left corner, click the Scoreboard tab. This displays a tile for each game currently underway. Click one to display up-to-date results.

# Creating an investment Watchlist

One of the great features of the Money app in Windows 10 is the ability to create a Watchlist that includes the investments that interest you most. This list can include stocks and other investments, and you can use it to easily track the latest valuations for your investments.

## Create a Watchlist

**1** Open the Money app and click Watchlist.

**2** Items currently on your watchlist are displayed. Click an item to view details about the item.

**3** Click the Add to Watchlist button.

**4** Type a company name or stock exchange abbreviation.

**5** Click a result to add it to your Watchlist.

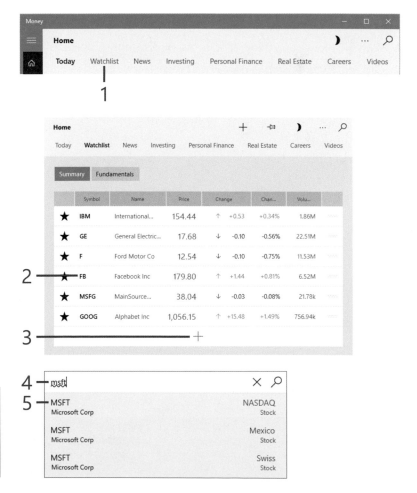

> **TIP** If keeping track of global currencies is important to your investment scheme, click the Currencies button in the navigation pane. Here, you can locate current values for major world currencies and view trends for currency valuations and exchange rates, such as USD to EURO.

# Viewing markets

The Money app can provide information about markets in the United States, which include stocks, commodities, bonds, and more. This information, which includes trends and up-to-the-minute rates for loans and credit cards, can be very useful when plotting your investment strategies.

## View stock markets

1  With the Money app open, click the Markets button.

2  Click the Summary tab to display major exchanges.

3  Click a stock exchange.

4  Use the scrollbar to review a detailed chart and statistics.

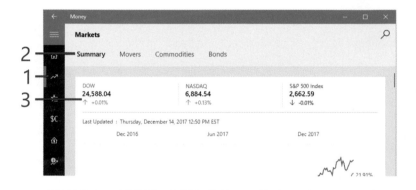

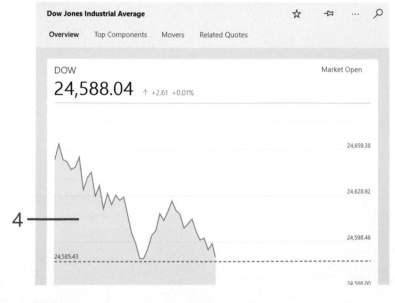

> **TIP**  Continue to scroll down the page for a market such as the Dow Jones to read recent news stories relevant to that exchange from various financial publications.

# Checking the weather

# 18

Whether you're wandering around your town where you live or visiting another country, being able to anticipate the weather helps you know what to wear, when to venture out, and how to cope with the vagaries of climate. The Weather app provides information about conditions in your current location or anywhere else of interest to you. You can view weather maps and historical data to spot trends. You can also get news about emerging weather patterns, from a local shower to more threatening conditions such as hurricanes or tornadoes.

This section offers step-by-step advice on how to make the most of the Weather app and use the data it provides for planning your day.

# Viewing the current weather

When you want to know what the day or week has in store for you weather-wise, the Weather app can be very useful. When you open the Weather app, you can view the weather information for the default location, or you can select other locations and check the current conditions for them.

## View weather details

1 Open the Weather app. Current weather conditions are displayed at the top of the main screen.

2 Scroll down to view daily and hourly forecasts, as well as other details like sunrise and sunset, and the phases of the moon.

**TIP** Here's another way to view your local weather report. If you have allowed access to your location (in the Action Center, by clicking the Location button), you enable Cortana to reflect the weather where your computer is located. With your Location turned on, Cortana's main panel then shows you the weather in your current location.

# Adding your favorite places

From your hometown to the towns where your business has branches or the nearest big city, you might want to include several locations that the Weather app tracks for you on a regular basis. Weather gives you the ability to designate one default location and an unlimited number of favorite places.

## Add a favorite place

1 With the Weather app open, click the Favorites button on the left.

2 You now see tiles for your previously entered favorite locations. Click a location to view that area's weather.

3 Scroll to the bottom of the favorites list and click the Add button

4 In the Search box, type a city name or postal code.

5 In the results list, click an item.

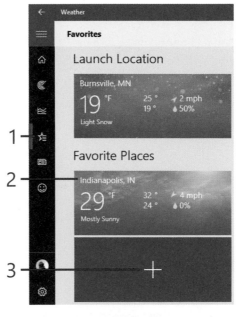

✓ **TIP** To remove a location, with Favorite Places displayed, right-click the location, and then, on the shortcut menu that opens, click Remove from Favorites.

# Changing your launch location

If you move to another city or are out of town on business for a few months, you want to change your default location—referred to in the Weather app as the *Launch Location*. You can manually type your location or allow Windows to detect your current location.

## Choose your default location

1 With the Weather app open, click the Settings button.

2 Scroll to the Launch Location section and make sure the Default Location option is selected.

3 Type a new location into the Launch Location box.

4 Click the Back button to return to the Weather app home screen.

---

✅ **TIP** To display a location's weather without adding it to Favorite Places, from the Places window, in the City Or ZIP Code search box, type a location. The weather for that location is displayed, but it isn't added to your Favorite Places.

✅ **TIP** If you'd rather use your current location as the default location, in the Launch Location settings, click Always Detect My Location.

# Choosing Fahrenheit or Celsius

If you're from Toronto, your temperature measurement of choice is likely Celsius. If you're from New York, Fahrenheit is your familiar measurement. In the Weather app, you can easily change how temperatures are presented to suit your preference.

## Make settings for temperature measurements

**1** With the Weather app open, click the Settings button.

**2** In the Show Temperature In section, click either the Fahrenheit or Celsius option.

**3** Click the Back button to return to the Weather app home screen.

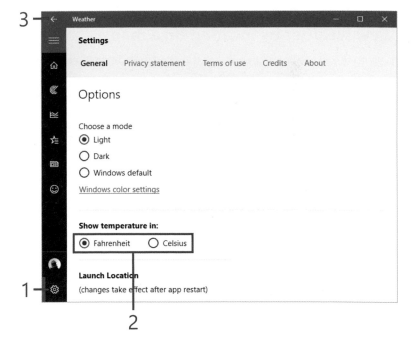

✓ **TIP** When you choose Fahrenheit or Celsius in the Launch Location settings, that measurement will be used for all your Favorite Places, regardless of the preferred measurement standard in that country.

# Viewing weather maps

In the Weather app, you can choose to view weather trends on a map. For example, with a weather map, you can move around the country spotting areas of colors that indicate rain or snow.

A legend along the bottom of the Maps window helps you to identify rain, snow, and other weather patterns.

## View weather by location on a map

1 With the Weather app open, click the Maps button on the left.

2 By default, you see a Radar Observation map of your current location, typically looped for the past several hours. Click the Pause button to pause the playback.

3 Click the Zoom In or Zoom Out button to view a more or less-detailed map.

**TRY THIS** To display different information on the Maps feature of Weather, click the Now Showing drop-down list (which displays Radar Observation by default) and choose from Temperature, Radar Observation, Radar Forecast, Precipitation, Satellite, or Cloud. (Not all options are available for all locations.)

# Finding weather news

News stories about impending weather can provide valuable details about the phenomena headed your way. The News section of the Weather app can produce articles on topics ranging from an upcoming heatwave or snowstorm to global warming.

## Read weather news

**1** With the Weather app open, click the News button.

**2** Scroll down to move through the stories.

**3** Click a story to read it.

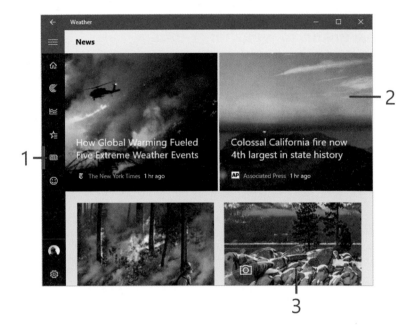

**TIP** To share a news story, open the story and click the Share button. You can opt to share via the Mail or Skype apps, or any social network to which you're connected.

# Displaying historical weather data

Weather trends can help you spot the way your year will go, weather-wise, or how the global climate is gradually changing. The Historical Weather feature of the Weather app provides graphs and statistics such as average rainfall and record-high temperatures.

## See a graph of weather trends

**1** With the Weather app open, click the Historical Weather button.

**2** Click to display temperature data.

**3** Click to display precipitation data.

**4** Click to display snowfall data.

**5** Click a different month in the chart to display historical data for that month.

**6** Scroll down to view more historical data.

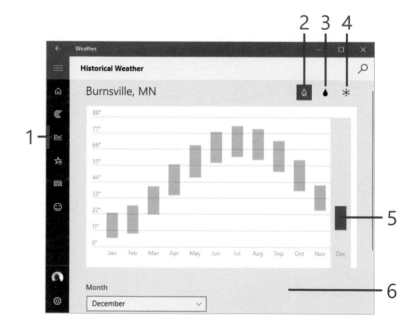

---

**✓ TIP** To view historical data for another location, enter that location into the Search box and select the location from the search results list.

---

# Using Maps

# 19

Using the Windows 10 Maps app, you can view locations around the globe. You can view your current location or any other specific location you're searching for, and then get directions from one location to another. You can take advantage of a variety of views of maps, from Aerial to Road views; Road views can also show traffic problems in real time. You can also use tools to tilt and rotate maps.

Also, you can use Cortana to designate favorite locations that will then be available in Maps Favorites, and view and manipulate three-dimensional maps of many cities around the world.

## In this section:

- Opening Maps and showing your location
- Getting directions in Maps
- Zooming in and out
- Changing map views
- Rotating and tilting maps
- Viewing Favorites
- Viewing cities in Aerial view

# Opening Maps and showing your location

The Maps app can locate where you are in the world and help you find nearby businesses, such as restaurants, or provide directions. To do this, though, you need to open the Maps app and allow it to find your location.

## Find your location in Maps

1 Click the Start button.

2 Click the Maps tile or menu item.

3 Click the Show My Location button.

4 The map is now recentered with your location highlighted.

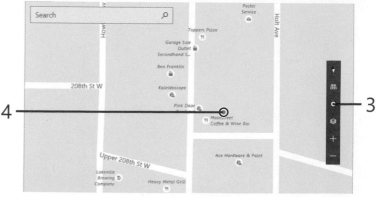

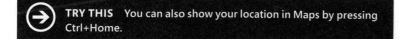

**TIP** You might have been prompted to turn on location tracking when you first set up Windows or opened the Maps app. If you chose not to do so at that time, you can turn on location-tracking capabilities by clicking the Action Center button, which is located on the taskbar, and then clicking Location. If you would like to turn off the feature when you're done with it, click Location again.

**TRY THIS** You can also show your location in Maps by pressing Ctrl+Home.

# Getting directions in Maps

People often use maps apps to get from point A to point B. The Maps app in Windows 10 has a very nice directions feature with which you can even generate step-by-step instructions on how to get to your destination along with an accompanying map, or display mileage and time estimates for your trip.

## Get directions

1   With the Maps app open, click the Directions button.

2   Click the A (Starting Point) box and then type a start location such as a street address, business name, or city.

3   Click the B (Destination) box and then type a destination (you can also select a recent location from the list in this view). You can enter a street address, city, and state, or desired location or landmark, such as the Mall of America or Wrigley Field.

4   Click Get Directions.

5   The Maps app often displays several sets of directions, with the recommended route displayed first. Click to select a given route; step by step directions are now displayed.

6   If you like, click Go to display a map with step-by-step directions.

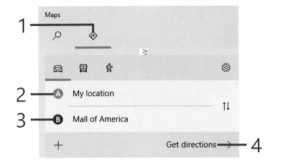

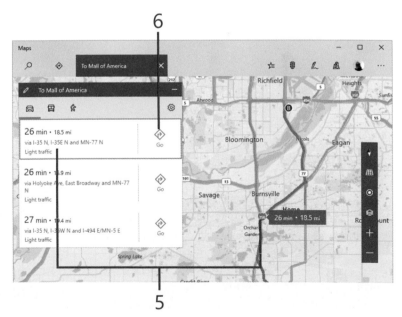

> **TIP** By default, directions are prepared with the assumption that you're traveling by car. To get directions if you're on foot or planning on taking public transit, click the icon with a walker or bus, respectively, which you can find directly above the From box.

> **TRY THIS** While entering start and ending locations in the Directions window, click the Route Options button and choose what to avoid, such as Traffic, Toll Roads, or Tunnels.

# Zooming in and out

The Maps app can give you a broad view of an area or a detailed view of individual streets and landmarks. The Zoom In and Zoom Out feature in Maps helps you find what you're looking for.

## Zoom in and out

**1** With the Maps app open and the Maps view displayed, click the Zoom In button.

**2** Click the Zoom Out button.

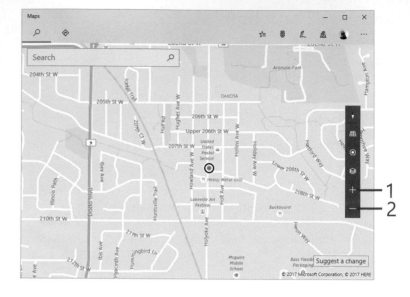

**TIP** You can also use a keyboard shortcut to zoom in or out. To zoom in press Ctrl+Plus Sign. To zoom out press Ctrl+Minus Sign.

**TRY THIS** If you have a touchscreen computer, you can zoom in by putting two fingers together, touching the screen, and then spreading them apart. To zoom out, place your fingers apart on the screen, and then pinch them together.

# Changing map views

The Maps app offers two viewing options: Aerial and Road. With each of these views, you can also show or hide a Traffic overlay, which shows traffic problems that you might want to avoid. (A green route means normal traffic flow; yellow means slower-than-normal traffic; red means substantial traffic delays.) You can also display details about those traffic problems to help you determine the best route for your travels, or view the picture from any nearby traffic cameras.

## Choose a map view

1  With the Maps app open and displaying a map for a single destination, click the Map Views button.

2  Click the alternate view from that which you're currently viewing; for example, click Aerial if you're viewing Road, and vice versa.

3  With Road selected, click the Traffic switch on.

(continued on next page)

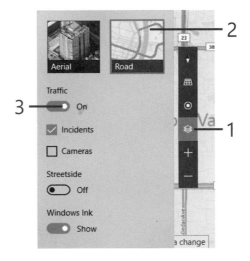

⚠ **TIP** To hide traffic information, click the Map Views button again, and then click Hide Traffic.

## Choose a map view *continued*

4 Click a traffic warning symbol to read the details of the incident.

5 Click a traffic camera symbol to view the picture from that location's traffic camera.

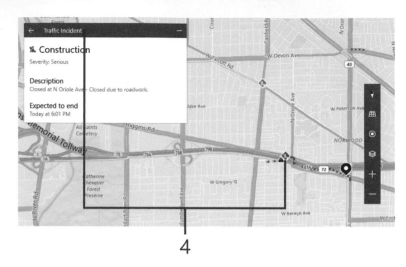

4

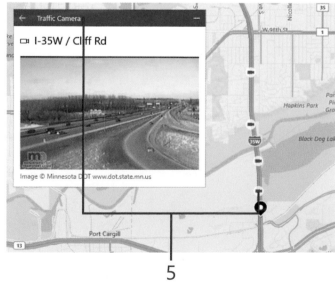

5

# Rotating and tilting maps

Two features of the Maps app can help you gain some perspective on what you're viewing. First, you can choose to rotate the map so that North is shown at the top of the map or rotate the map clockwise or counterclockwise. Second, you can tilt the map display up or down so that rather than seeing the view as if from directly above, you see it at an angle, and items on the map seem to be fading off into the distance.

## Change map angles

1   With the Maps app open and a map displayed, click the Rotate North to Top button. This reorients the map to a normal north/south orientation.

2   Click either the Rotate Counterclockwise or Rotate Clockwise button to rotate the map away from the normal north/south orientation.

3   Click the Tilt button to tilt the map down. To tilt the map back up, click the Tilt button again.

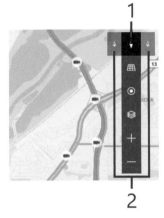

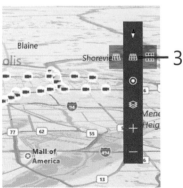

> **TIP**  To further broaden the angle of tilt on a map, click the Tilt Up or Tilt Down control repeatedly (to a maximum of three shifts of tilt). To return to the zero-tilt view, click the center Tilt button.

# Viewing Favorites

The Maps app enables you to create favorite places that you may revisit. After you add a favorite place, the next time you open the Maps app your favorites will be available when you click the Favorites button. You can then display directions and information about those favorites.

## Display favorite directions

**1** With the Maps app open, click the Favorites button.

**2** To add a new favorite place, click Add a Place.

**3** Enter or click the name or address of that location.

**4** Click a favorite place to display that place on the map and information about that place in the panel.

> **TIP** To delete a Favorite, display Favorites, and then right-click the one that you want to remove. On the shortcut menu that opens, click Delete. .

# Viewing cities in Aerial view

With the Maps app, you can display a three-dimensional Aerial view of many cities around the world. When you display a city in Aerial view, you can use the tilt and rotate tools on the right end of the toolbar to manipulate the view.

## See select cities in Aerial view

**1** With the Maps app open, click the 3D Cities button.

**2** Click a city.

*(continued on next page)*

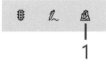

1

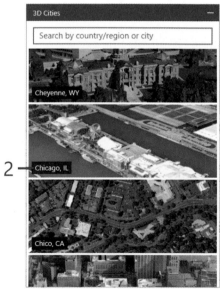

2

---

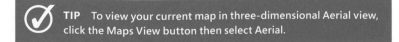

**TIP** To view your current map in three-dimensional Aerial view, click the Maps View button then select Aerial.

## See select cities in Aerial view _continued_

**3** Click and drag your mouse to move around the city. Use your mouse's scroll button or the Zoom In/Zoom Out controls to zoom in and out of the city map.

**4** Click the Maps View button and then select Road to exit the Aerial view.

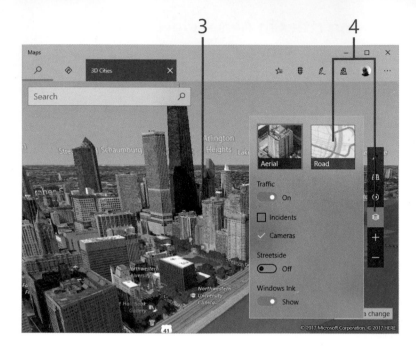

# Playing with Xbox games

# 20

People have been playing games on computers for many years now. Today, games have added many features such as the ability to play with others online and to track your gaming achievements. Also, you can use an avatar (an illustration that represents a person) as the persona that you present to other gamers or choose a picture, called a *gamerpic*.

The Xbox app is preinstalled in Windows 10. You don't need to own an Xbox console to play games on your computer using this app. If you do own an Xbox, your gaming achievements will be tracked across your devices.

## In this section:

- Downloading games
- Adding friends
- Switching between an avatar and a gamerpic
- Playing games
- Inviting friends to play games
- Sending a message to a friend
- Recording game screens

## Downloading games

There is a wide assortment of computer games out there, from children's games to Solitaire and action games. Some games are free; others you must purchase from the Microsoft Store.

### Get new games

**1** Click the Store icon on the Windows taskbar or Start menu.

**2** Click the Games tab.

**3** Scroll down to look at suggested games in categories such as Top Games or Featured Games.

**4** Click a game to view details about it.

*(continued on next page)*

While you can enter the Microsoft Store from the Xbox app, it's quicker and easier to open the Store app directly to do your game shopping.

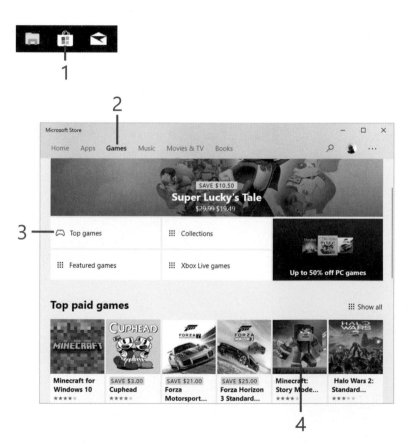

## Get new games   *continued*

**5**   To download a free game, click the Get button.

**6**   To purchase a paid game, click the Buy button and follow the onscreen instructions to complete your purchase.

## Adding friends

Although you can play games on your own on your computer, in the gaming world you can also add friends with whom you can play online games. After you add friends, you can then invite a friend to play a game, compare achievements, and more.

### Add a friend

1  With the Xbox app open, click Friends List.

2  In the Find People or Clubs box, type a name.

3  Click the Search button.

4  The Xbox app displays a matching player. If this is the person you want, click Add Friend.

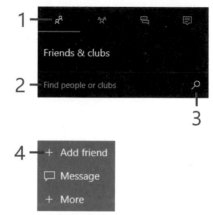

---

**TIP**  To make changes to your friendship, click the Friends List button, click the friend you want to edit, click the More button in the friend's pane, and then click Change Friendship. In the window that opens, you can move a friend to Favorites, share your real name with that person, or remove the friend entirely.

# Switching between an avatar and a gamerpic

An avatar is an illustration that represents your gaming persona to others. Xbox offers the option of using an avatar or a *gamerpic*. A gamerpic is a small circle containing an illustration or other graphic representation. You are assigned a generic avatar by default, but you can change to a gamerpic with a simple procedure.

## Choose an avatar or gamerpic

1   With the Xbox app open, click your Gamer button in the navigation pane.

2   Click Customize.

3   Click the Edit icon next to your avatar.

4   Click a gamerpic preview.

5   Click Done.

> **TIP**   You can also choose a picture stored on your computer as your avatar. In Step 4, click Choose a Custom Picture and then select the picture you want to use.

# Playing games

After you own a game, you can begin to play. Of course, games vary widely, from Solitaire to car-racing games, and they all have different features. Each game has its own controls and settings, but the basic process of finding and playing a game is the same.

## Play a game

1 With Xbox open, click the My Games button in the navigation pane.

2 You now see all the games installed on your computer. Click Play adjacent to a game to play it.

  **TIP** If you want to connect to an Xbox console that might already contain games, connect your Xbox console to your PC, and then click the Connection button in the navigation pane and select your Xbox console from the list. If the device is connected to your computer, it will be detected. If it's not, provide the console's IP address, and then click Connect.

  **TIP** To stop playing a game if it opens in a separate window, in the top-right corner of the window, click the Close button.

## Inviting friends to play games

Even though playing a game on your own can be fun, sometimes it's more fun to play against an opponent. After you've added friends who have the same game you have, you can invite them to play with you via an online connection.

### Invite a friend to play

**1** With Xbox open, click the Friends List button.

**2** Click a friend to display details.

**3** Click Invite.

**4** Click Invite to Party

**5** Your friend receives a message and then can click to join the game. You're notified that the invitation has been sent; click OK.

> ✓ **TIP** A gaming party can involve just two players or multiple players.

# Sending a message to a friend

Having gamer friends makes your gaming experience richer. You can even use tools in Xbox to communicate with your friends, sending them messages about getting together for a game or to boast about your latest scores.

## Send a message

1   With Xbox open, click the Messages button.

2   Click the New Message button.

3   You see a list of your Xbox friends. Click the friend or friends you want to message

4   Selected friends are added to the To box. Click Add when done selecting recipients.

*(continued on next page)*

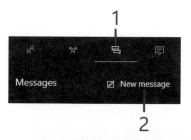

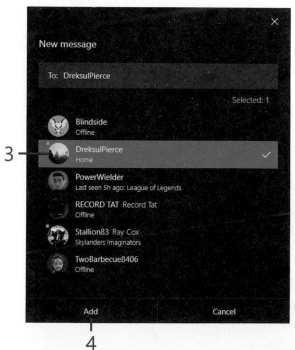

## Send a message *continued*

**5** Click the Enter Message box and type your message.

**6** Click Send.

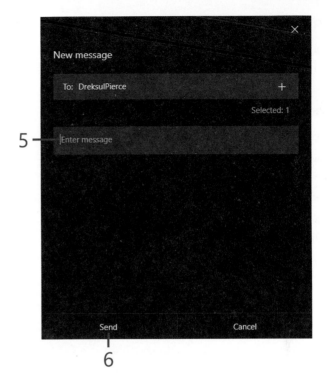

## Recording game screens

If you think you're about to score a major win in a game, you might want to record your gaming session and share it with like-minded gamers. Recording is easy to do, and it helps you improve your scores over time by viewing your past mistakes and achievements.

### Record and share games

1   Play a game in Xbox.

2   While you're playing the game, press the Windows logo key+Alt+R to begin recording; a recording counter displays.

3   Press the Windows logo key+Alt+R again to stop recording.

4   Back in the Xbox app, Click the Game DVR button in the navigation pane.

5   Click a recording to play it.

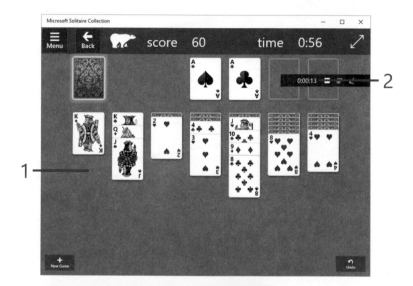

TIP   When you play a recording, you can use editing tools to trim or rename the clip, and then share it with others.

# Adding and working with other devices

# 21

Windows 10 can work with various devices such as printers, smart TVs, and Bluetooth-enabled peripherals (e.g., a mouse or keyboard). To do this, you need to configure certain settings and connections, which often involves following the guided instructions in something called a *wizard*. For example, you can specify settings to manage the attributes and capabilities of a printer or scanner or connected devices such as a mouse. You can also examine the properties of devices using Device Manager and update *device drivers* (small software programs with which Windows 10 connects to and communicates with various devices).

If you no longer need to have a device connected to your computer, you can remove it and its driver software.

## In this section:

- Adding a printer or scanner
- Configuring printer settings
- Adding a connected device
- Using Bluetooth devices
- Viewing device properties in Device Manager
- Updating device drivers
- Removing a device

# Adding a printer or scanner

Windows 10 provides a unique procedure for adding printers and scanners through the Devices portion of Settings. Windows usually detects printers or scanners through a connected network or physical connection; if it doesn't, you can manually add a device.

## Add a printer

**1** From the Settings window, click Devices.

**2** Click Printers & Scanners in the left pane.

**3** Click Add a Printer or Scanner.

*(continued on next page)*

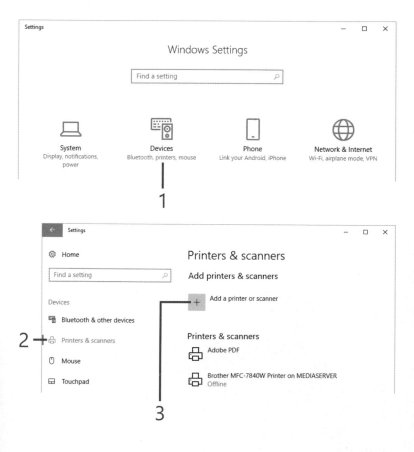

> ✓ **TIP**  If the printer you want to add doesn't appear in the Add a Printer results, click The Printer That I Want Isn't Listed, and then follow instructions to locate older printers (those that don't have plug-and-play technology through which Windows can identify them) or provide more information to help Windows locate the printer.

> ✓ **TIP**  Many new printers can connect wirelessly to your computer via Wi-Fi. Click Show Wi-Fi Direct Printers to show available wireless printers, and then click the one you want to add and follow the onscreen instructions.

## Add a printer *continued*

**4** In the list that appears, click the printer that you want to add.

**5** Click Add Device.

# Configuring printer settings

You can configure several settings when printing a document from within an application. For example, you can select the printer to which you want to print, choose which pages in the document to print, set up page collation, page orientation, and margins. The settings you can make vary depending on the printer that you're using.

## Choose how to print

1  Open a productivity app, such as WordPad, and then click File.

2  Click Print.

3  In the Print dialog box that opens, select the printer you want to use from the Select Printer list.

4  Click Pages and specify a page range to print; for example, type **1-8** (or click All to print all the pages in the document).

5  In the Number of Copies box, click the up or down arrows or type a number directly in the box to set the number of copies.

6  Click Print.

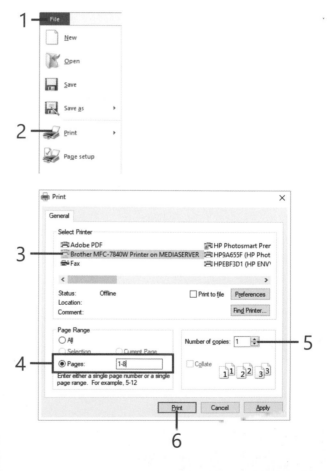

> **TIP**   If you print a document to OneNote, you essentially send a copy of it to the online document management system where you can then work with it or share it.

> **TRY THIS**   To make further printer settings in the Print dialog box, click the Preferences button. Depending on your printer's features, you can choose options such as the size of paper to print on, print quality, color settings, and so on.

# Using Bluetooth devices

Bluetooth is a technology with which you can connect one Bluetooth-enabled device to another when they are within close proximity. For example, you might connect to your smartphone or a Bluetooth keyboard. To use Bluetooth, you must make the device *discoverable* and then pair your computer with it.

## Pair your computer with a Bluetooth device

**1** From the Settings window, click Devices.

**2** Click Bluetooth & Other Devices.

**3** Click the Bluetooth switch to turn the feature on if it's off. (It should be on by default.)

**4** Click Add Bluetooth or Other Device.

*(continued on next page)*

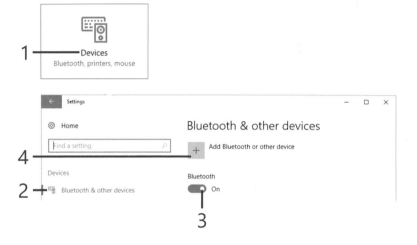

## Pair your computer with a Bluetooth device *continued*

**5** In the Add a Device panel, click Bluetooth.

**6** Windows now searches for discoverable Bluetooth devices. Click a recognized Bluetooth device to pair it with your computer. Follow any onscreen instructions to complete the connection.

5 —

6 —

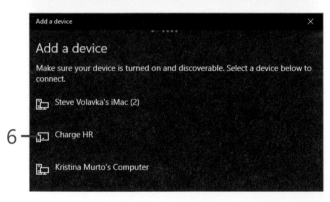

# Adding other connected devices

You can connect other types of devices, both wired and wireless. In most instances Windows 10 automatically recognizes the device when connected, but in some situations you might need to add the device manually. Windows first detects the device and then takes you through steps to set it up.

## Set up a connected device

**1** From the Settings window, click Devices.

**2** Click Bluetooth & Other Devices. (Or, if you're connecting a printer or scanner, click Printers and Scanners.)

**3** Click Add Bluetooth or Other Device.

*(continued on next page)*

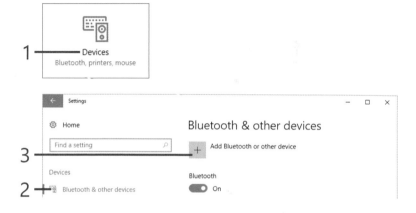

---

**TIP** You might be asked to enter a PIN or password for the connected device. This should be available on the device itself, or in the device's instruction manual.

## Set up a connected device  *continued*

4   In the Add a Device panel, click the type of device you're adding—Bluetooth, Wireless Display or Dock, or Everything Else.

5   Windows now scans for discoverable devices. Click the device you want to set up and follow the onscreen instructions to complete the installation.

4 —

5 —

## Viewing device properties in Device Manager

Device Manager is a Windows feature that makes it possible for you to view all devices connected to or installed on your computer, such as a keyboard or graphics controller, and examine their properties. Being able to access this information can help you troubleshoot problems with your computer.

### View information about your devices

**1** Right-click the Start menu.

**2** Click Device Manager.

*(continued on next page)*

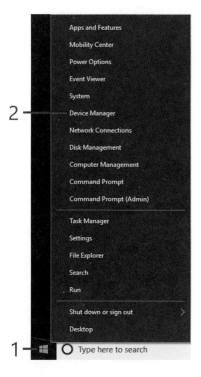

## View information about your devices *continued*

3  Double-click a category such as Keyboards.

4  Right-click a device.

5  On the shortcut menu that opens, click Properties.

6  Click various tabs to view details about the device.

7  Click OK to close the dialog box.

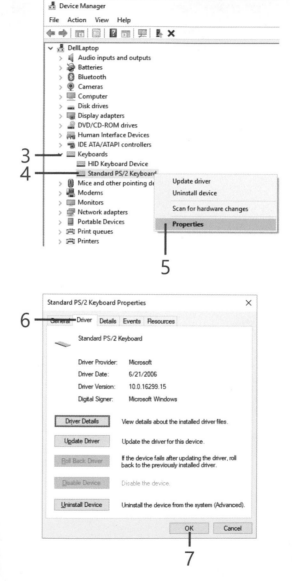

# Updating device drivers

To connect devices to your computer, you must install *device drivers*. These small programs give Windows the information it needs to communicate with the devices and provide the appropriate instructions to them. Device drivers are regularly updated to improve their functionality or add security features. For that reason, it's useful to know how to update your drivers.

## Search for updated driver software

**1** With the Device Manager window open (see the previous task), right-click a device.

**2** On the shortcut menu that opens, click Update Driver.

**3** Click Search Automatically for Updated Driver Software.

**4** Click the device model for which you want the updated driver, and then follow the onscreen instructions to install the new driver.

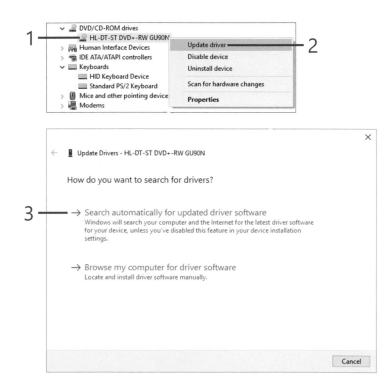

**TIP**  If you believe the device driver software might be located on your computer or a storage drive, in step 3 you can click Browse My Computer for Driver Software.

# Removing a device

If you are no longer using a device, you might want to remove it from your computer. This makes lists of available devices shorter so that you can more easily manage active devices, and it removes unneeded driver software from your computer, freeing up memory.

## Remove a device from your computer

1 With the Device Manager window open, right-click the name of the device that you want to remove.

2 On the shortcut menu that opens, click Uninstall Device.

3 Click Uninstall to confirm that you want to remove the device.

> ✓ **TIP** Some devices offer you the option of disabling them rather than uninstalling them. If you think you might want to use the device again in the future, in step 2 choose the Disable Device command.

# Working with OneDrive

# 22

Microsoft OneDrive is an online service for storing content and sharing that content with others. When you first set up Windows 10, you'll be asked to also set up OneDrive, which requires you to be signed in with your Microsoft account.

OneDrive is integrated into apps such as Microsoft Outlook and Office 365, and even mobile apps for Windows smartphones so that you can save documents directly to it and access your content from different devices. With Windows 10, you have a version of OneDrive on your computer and another online version that synchronizes (backs up) your content to the cloud on a regular basis when you go online.

You can go to OneDrive online and create folders, upload content, share that content, and search through it. You can also remove content from OneDrive. With a Microsoft account, you can get to OneDrive through Outlook.com, or you can go to *onedrive.live.com* to work with your files.

The first time you go to OneDrive, you need to follow a few simple steps to configure and activate your OneDrive account.

## In this section:

- Navigating OneDrive
- Creating a new folder
- Uploading files to OneDrive
- Searching for a file in OneDrive
- Creating documents with Office Online
- Sharing folders
- Renaming files and folders
- Deleting files and folders
- Synchronizing Files On-Demand

# Navigating OneDrive

You access the version of OneDrive stored on your computer as a folder in File Explorer, where you can store documents ready to synchronize with the online version of OneDrive. The real work of sharing and managing files with OneDrive is handled online, where you can access your content from any computer, tablet, or smartphone, from anywhere.

## Navigate OneDrive from File Explorer

1  On your computer, open File Explorer and click OneDrive in the navigation pane.

2  Double-click to open a folder.

3  Double-click to open a file.

4  To manage your files, click any file and then click the appropriate option on File Explorer's Home ribbon.

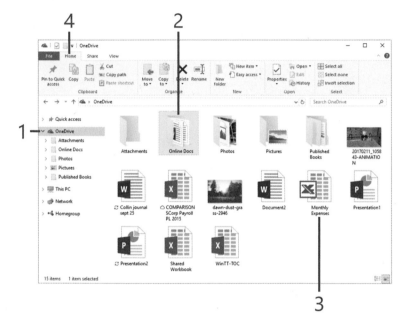

## Navigate OneDrive online

**1** Open your web browser and, in the address bar, type **onedrive.live. com**, and then press Enter. (If prompted, sign into your account with your Windows username/email address and password.)

**2** Files should be selected by default in the navigation pane. If not, click Files.

**3** Click a folder to display its contents.

**4** Click Sort.

**5** Click the appropriate criteria for sorting, such as Size.

**6** Click Photos.

**7** Scroll to view additional photos.

**8** Click the Apps button.

**9** Click Files to return to the Files screen.

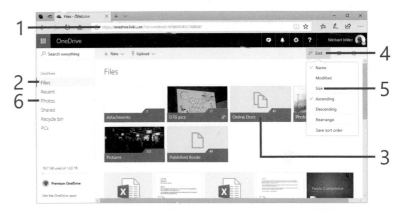

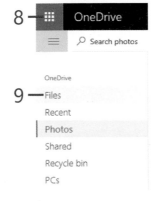

 **TIP** Click PCs in the navigation pane to see any computers that have access to your OneDrive.

# Creating a new folder

In addition to working with folders that are automatically backed up to OneDrive from your computer, you can create a new folder in OneDrive and then upload files to it. This allows you to create your own folders of content online that don't necessarily replicate what's stored on your computer.

## Create a folder in OneDrive

1 With OneDrive open to the Files screen, click New.

2 Click Folder.

3 Type a folder name.

4 Click Create.

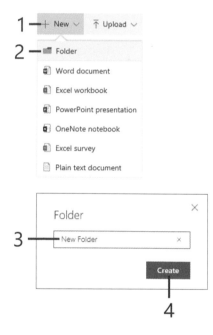

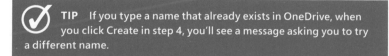
**TIP** If you type a name that already exists in OneDrive, when you click Create in step 4, you'll see a message asking you to try a different name.

# Uploading files to OneDrive

Although your Windows 10 computer automatically backs up selected folders and files to OneDrive, there might be times when you want to upload specific content to an online folder to share it with others. For example, you might want to create a folder called "Third-Quarter Budget" in OneDrive and only upload to it those spreadsheets and other documents that pertain to the third quarter, even though no such folder exists on your computer.

## Upload a file or folder

1   With OneDrive open to the Files screen, click a folder, or create a new folder (see the previous task), and then click Upload.

2   Click Files.

3   In the Open dialog box, locate and select the file or files that you want to upload.

4   Click Open.

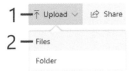

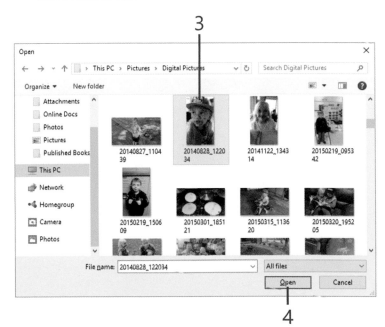

**TIP**   OneDrive comes with 5 GB of free storage (if you subscribe to Office 365, the limit is 1 TB), but you can buy more. On the OneDrive title bar, click the Settings button (the cog icon) and choose Options. Then, click the Buy More Storage button and follow the directions to acquire more storage. Note that you can also get more storage by referring somebody to OneDrive and through various loyalty and app-related promotions.

# Searching for a file in OneDrive

When you have many files and folders in OneDrive online, you need a method to search for the specific items you want, just as File Explorer helps you find content on your computer's hard disk and storage drives. OneDrive offers a Search feature that you can use to do just that.

## Search for content

**1** With OneDrive open, click within the Search Everything box.

**2** Type a word or phrase and then press Enter.

**3** In the search results, click a file or folder.

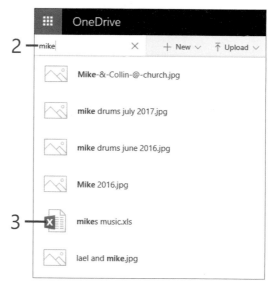

**TIP** To change views from a graphic representation of files and folders to a simple list, on the right side of the Sort button, click the View Options button.

## Sharing folders

One of the most useful features of OneDrive is the option to share large files with others. Because email attachments are often limited by file size, sharing by using a service such as One-Drive makes it possible for you to share files that you otherwise could not send by email. You share by inviting people via an email to view the file. When you do, you can choose whether those people can simply view the files or actually edit them.

### Share OneDrive content with others

1  With OneDrive online open and a folder whose contents you want to share open, click Share.

2  Click Allow Editing if you want to give the people with whom you're sharing permission to edit content.

3  Click Email.

4  Type an email address.

5  Add an accompanying message, if you like.

6  Click Share.

> **TIP**  If you'd rather create your own email and embed a link to your files, in the left panel of the Share window, click Get A Link, and then click the Copy button. You can then paste this link into your email or text message.

# Creating documents with Office Online

From within OneDrive, you can create documents that are saved there using Office Online. This suite includes Microsoft Word, Excel, and PowerPoint. You can also create OneNote and Sway files. This capability can be very handy when you're using a computer or tablet that doesn't have Office apps installed.

## Create a Word Online document

**1** With OneDrive open, click the Apps button.

**2** Click Word.

**3** Select a template for your document.

*(continued on next page)*

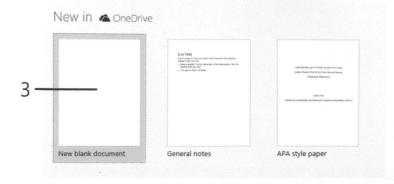

## Create a Word Online document continued

**4** Type your document contents.

**5** Use the tools on the various tabs to format and organize your content.

**6** Click File.

**7** Click Save As.

**8** Click Save As to save the document to OneDrive.

**9** Click the folder where you want to save the file.

**10** Click Save.

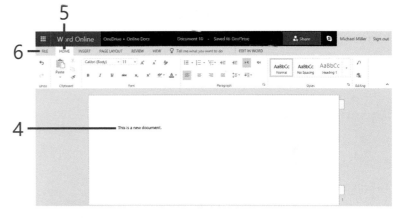

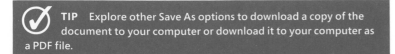

**TIP** Explore other Save As options to download a copy of the document to your computer or download it to your computer as a PDF file.

# Renaming files and folders

Just as you find it useful to rename files and folders in File Explorer, so you might need to do the same in OneDrive. As project names, company names, and more items change in your life, the ability to rename content in your online storage service helps you keep up to date.

## Rename a file or folder

**1** Locate a file or folder in OneDrive and right-click it.

**2** On the shortcut menu that opens, click Rename.

**3** Type a new name.

**4** Click Save.

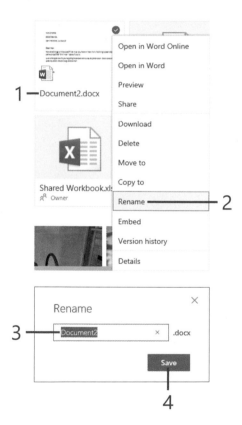

---

 **TIP** You can't rename a file or folder with a name that's already in use. You must use unique names when renaming files or folders.

# Deleting files and folders

Although 5 GB of storage might sound impressive, you might find that it fills up faster than you thought it would. To save space, you can periodically delete files and folders that you no longer need.

## Delete content

1  With OneDrive open, in the top-right corner of one or more files or folders that you want to remove, select the round checkmark.

2  Click Delete.

3  If you change your mind about deleting the item or items, in the confirmation message that appears, click Undo All.

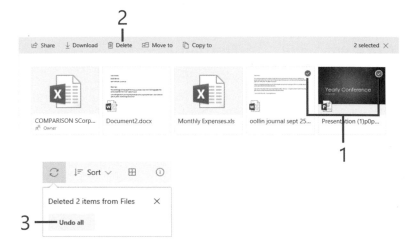

# Synchronizing Files On-Demand

The Windows 10 Fall Creators Update introduced a feature called Files On-Demand that lets you work directly with files stored online with OneDrive, without first having to download those files to your computer. Files On-Demand lets you access the same files from multiple computers and devices, and have all your work show up on all your devices. When you make a change in a file on one computer or device, all the other versions of the file will automatically reflect that change.

## Work with Files On-Demand

**1** From within File Explorer, click OneDrive.

**2** View the On-Demand status of each file from the Status column in Details view, or next to the file name in any other view. Online Only files are only available online in OneDrive; Locally Available files are stored on your computer; and Always Available files are stored online but can be edited on your computer or other devices.

**3** To change the On-Demand status of any file, right-click that file.

**4** Select View Online to make a file Always Available.

**5** Select Always Keep on This Device to make a file Locally Available.

**6** Click Free Up Space to make a file Online Only.

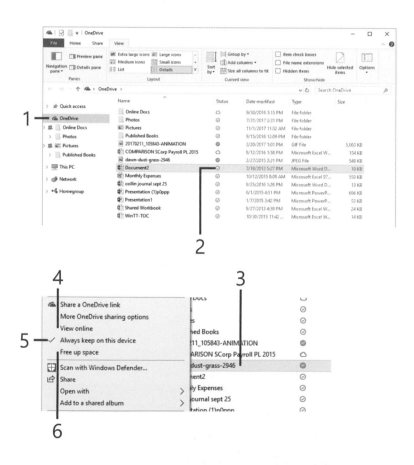

# Maintaining and protecting your computer

# 23

## In this section:

- Optimizing your hard disk
- Using Disk Cleanup
- Obtaining updates
- Resetting your computer
- Working with Windows Defender
- Running Windows Defender updates and scans
- Configuring Windows Firewall
- Changing Location settings

Windows 10 provides several handy tools to help keep your computer performing optimally and with the most up-to-date security. You can perform a disk cleanup to remove bits of data that are no longer being used, including temporary files. When you instruct Windows 10 to optimize your hard disk, it takes noncontiguous pieces—or, fragments— and organizes them to make it easier for Windows to locate items, which improves your computer's performance. (Note that if your computer is equipped with a solid-state drive, you won't run into these issues.)

You can perform regular updates to ensure that you have the most current security features for Windows 10 to protect your computer. Also, you can configure Windows Defender and Windows Firewall—features that help protect your computer and data. If you're experiencing serious problems with your computer, you can reset it to an earlier version of Windows or restore factory settings—settings that were in place when you purchased your computer or upgraded the operating system.

Finally, Location tracking is turned on by default in Windows 10, but you might prefer to turn off this feature to prevent thieves from knowing where your computer is.

## Optimizing your hard disk

When you save documents, pictures, and other types of files, Windows 10 stores them on your hard disk in bits and pieces that might or might not be contiguous. That is, the pieces of data that make up your report on bird migration patterns might be located all over your drive, not stored all together in one place.

Every time you open the document, Windows must look across your entire hard disk to reassemble all these file fragments. Optimizing helps to improve your computer's performance by organizing these pieces such that they are contiguous on your hard drive, and therefore quicker to access.

### Run the optimization process

**1** In the Cortana Search box, type **optimize**.

**2** Click Defragment and Optimize Drives.

*(continued on next page)*

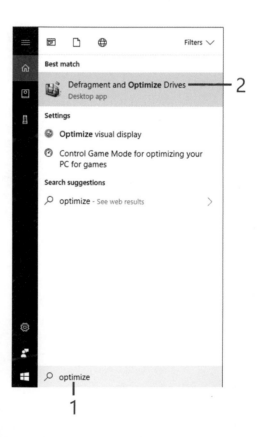

> **✓ TIP**  If you prefer, prior to optimizing, you can analyze your computer to see whether it needs it at all. Just click the Analyze button before clicking the Optimize button and review the report that's generated.

> **✓ TIP**  You can click Change Settings in the Optimize Drives dialog box and set a scheduled optimization on certain drives at a regular time interval, such as every week.

## Run the optimization process  *continued*

**3** Click the drive that you want to optimize. This is typically Windows (C:).

**4** Click Optimize.

**5** When the status shows that the optimizing process is complete, click Close.

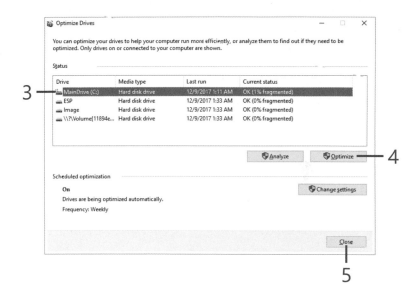

# Using Disk Cleanup

When you use your computer for various tasks, your hard disk begins to fill up with lots of information that could be in the form of files, temporary files created as you browse the Internet, old software programs, and so on. Disk Cleanup looks for corrupt data, temporary files, and unused bits and pieces on your hard disk and deletes them, freeing up space that you could be using for other things.

## Clear up space using Disk Cleanup

1   In the Cortana Search box, type **disk cleanup**.

2   Click Disk Cleanup.

3   Select the check boxes to the left of any types of files or folders that you want to remove.

4   Click Clean Up System Files.

5   Click OK.

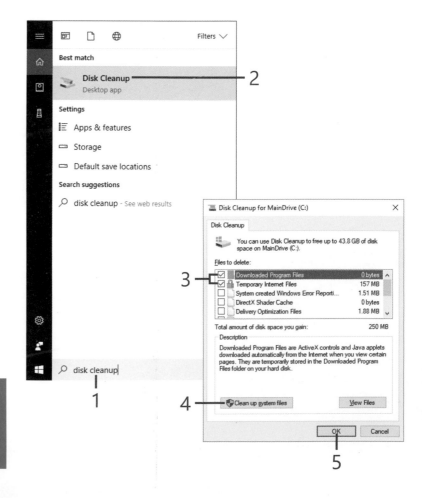

> ✓ **TIP**   If you're concerned that Disk Cleanup might delete files you need, you can view the files that Windows suggests and clear the check mark (deselect) for those that you don't want removed before proceeding. To examine the files, in the Disk Cleanup dialog box, click the View Files button.

# Obtaining updates

Microsoft makes updates available from time to time to fix bugs or security gaps created by the latest attack technique used to infiltrate your computer. It's important to get these updates to protect your computer and data. With Windows 10, which will rely on frequent changes to add or modify app features as well as its operating system, updating becomes even more important. Windows automatically checks for updates on a regular basis, but you also can manually check if you prefer.

## Run Windows Update

**1** In Settings, click Update & Security.

**2** Click Windows Update on the left side.

**3** Click Check for Updates. If updates are available, Windows downloads them. After the download is complete, click Install Now to install the update.

**TIP** When updates are performed, Windows often restarts to finalize the changes. If you are bothered by your computer restarting with little notice, under Windows Updates, click the Restart Options link. Then, on the next screen, turn on the Schedule a Time switch and select the time you want your computer to restart—typically during the middle of the night when you're not using your PC.

# Resetting your computer

When you experience serious problems with your computer, and you see no way to solve them, you might need to reset your computer. With the reset process, you can choose whether you want to retain your files or get rid of them, and then you can reinstall Windows. Resetting can remove apps you've installed or revert any settings that you've configured that might have corrupted Windows, and thus you start with a clean slate.

## Repair problems with a reset

**1**  In the Settings window, click Update & Security.

**2**  Click Recovery.

**3**  In the Reset This PC section, click Get Started.

*(continued on next page)*

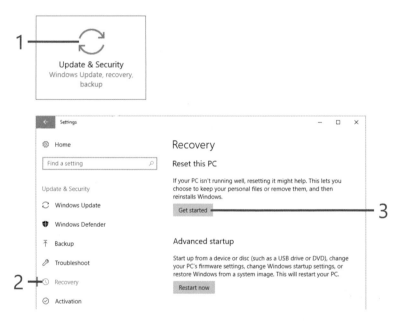

✓ **TIP**  If you decide to reset your computer while removing all your files, consider first backing up all your files on an external storage device such as a USB stick, or saving them to the cloud. If you are removing apps, also ensure that you have a way to reinstall those that you need after the reset, either from DVDs or the Internet.

## Repair problems with a reset *continued*

**4** Click a box to select the option you want for your reset.

Your options are:

- Keep my files (resets Windows to original factory condition without deleting any files)

- Remove everything (resets your entire computer to original factory condition, deleting all files on your PC)

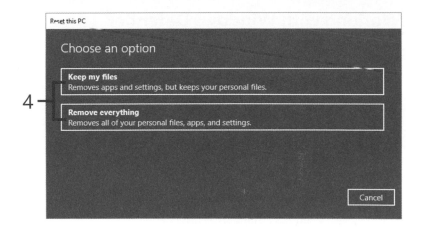

# Working with Windows Defender

One of the dangers of connecting to the Internet is the possibility of unintentionally installing malware on your computer, which can damage its contents or spy on the activities of the user. You can buy third-party security applications, but your first line of defense is to use the anti-malware program built into

Windows 10 called Windows Defender. You can turn off Windows Defender (though it's not recommended); if you do, after a period of time, Windows will turn it on again because it's that important that you have this protection.

## Manage Windows Defender settings

**1** From the Settings window, click Update & Security, and then click Windows Defender.

**2** Click Open Windows Defender Security Center.

**3** The main screen displays the status of key security operations, including Device Performance & Health, Firewall & Network Protection, and App & Browser Control. Click Virus & Threat Protection.

*(continued on next page)*

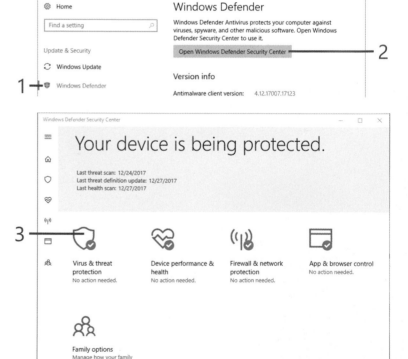

## Manage Windows Defender settings *continued*

**4** To change scan settings, click Virus & Threat Protection Settings.

**5** Make sure that Real-Time Protection and Cloud-Delivered Protection are both switched on.

**6** Scroll down to Controlled Folder Access and click that switch on. (This protects you from ransomware attacks that try to hold your data hostage until you pay a ransom.)

**7** In the Exclusions section, click Add or Remove Exclusions.

*(continued on next page)*

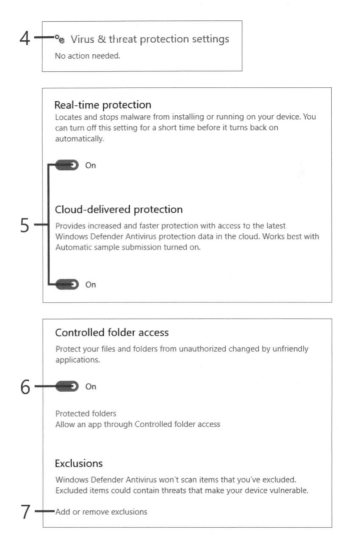

4 ——  Virus & threat protection settings

No action needed.

**Real-time protection**

Locates and stops malware from installing or running on your device. You can turn off this setting for a short time before it turns back on automatically.

On

**Cloud-delivered protection**

5 —— Provides increased and faster protection with access to the latest Windows Defender Antivirus protection data in the cloud. Works best with Automatic sample submission turned on.

On

**Controlled folder access**

Protect your files and folders from unauthorized changed by unfriendly applications.

6 —— On

Protected folders
Allow an app through Controlled folder access

**Exclusions**

Windows Defender Antivirus won't scan items that you've excluded. Excluded items could contain threats that make your device vulnerable.

7 —— Add or remove exclusions

## Manage Windows Defender settings *continued*

**8** Click Add an Exclusion.

**9** Click the type of item you want to exclude from your scans, such as File or Folder.

**10** Locate the item to exclude.

**11** Click Select Folder.

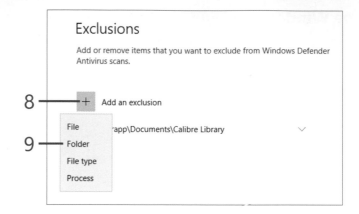

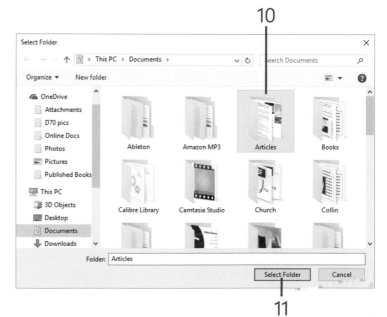

---

**TIP** If you find an instance of malware on your computer, you can help make Windows Defender stronger by sending a sample to Microsoft. To do so, in the Windows Defender Security Center, ensure that the Automatic Sample Submission switch is set to on.

# Running Windows Defender updates and scans

When Windows Defender is activated, which it is by default, it will protect your computer automatically. However, if you want to run a manual update of virus definitions and scan—for example, to determine if you have visited a questionable website or downloaded a suspicious file—you can do so from the Windows Defender Security Center.

## Run manual updates and scans

**1** From the Windows Defender Security Center, click Virus & Threat Protection.

**2** Click the Quick Scan button to perform a manual scan.

**3** Click Protection Updates.

**4** Click Check for Updates to manually check for and download any available virus updates.

1—

2—

3—

4

# Configuring Windows Firewall

A firewall is a tool that stops suspicious software from being downloaded to your computer when you go online. A firewall acts as a barrier between your computer and the Internet, but you can set up exclusions to allow certain content to download.

Windows Firewall is built into Windows 10. Note that these steps apply to a home network; if you are working on a company network, your administrator will deal with firewall settings for all users.

## Protect your computer using Windows Firewall

1 Open the Windows Defender Security Center and click Firewall & Network Protection.

2 Make sure that the firewall is turned on for all three types of networks—domain network, private network, and public network. (If the firewall is not turned on, click that type of network, and then click on the firewall on the next screen.)

3 Click Allow an App Through Firewall.

*(continued on next page)*

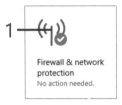

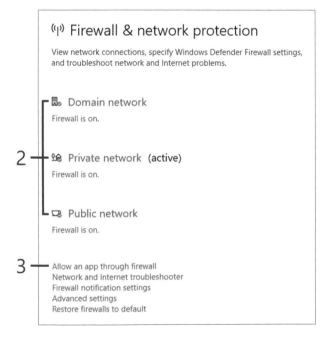

# Protect your computer using
# Windows Firewall *continued*

**4** All Internet-based apps are listed in the Allowed Apps panel. Click Change Settings.

**5** Uncheck an app to block it, or check an app to allow it through the firewall.

**6** Click OK.

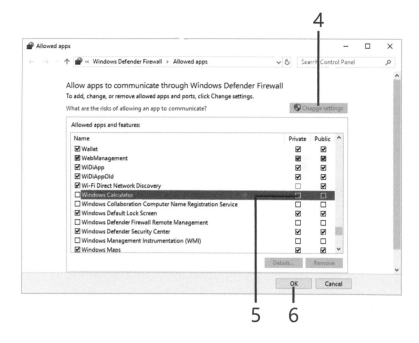

# Changing Location settings

It's possible for certain applications to locate you geographically. Sometimes this is helpful, as with the Maps app that can provide directions from your current location to a destination (for more information on this app, read Section 19, "Using Maps"). However, some apps use your location to sell you items, and some criminals use your location for identity theft or to commit offline crimes, including stealing your computer itself. If you prefer, you can change your Location settings so that your computer's whereabouts are not visible to others.

## Choose whether to share your location

**1** In Windows Settings, click Privacy.

**2** Click Location.

**3** Under Location For This Device Is On (or Off) click the Change button, and then click the Location For This Device switch to change the current setting if you want.

**4** To stop apps and services from asking for your location, click the Location Service switch to On if it's not already.

> ✓ **TIP** To quickly turn Location services off, click the Action Center button, and then click the Location button. Repeat this procedure to turn it on again.

> → **TRY THIS** To allow only certain apps to request your location, scroll down in the Privacy window, and then, in the Choose Apps That Can Use Your Location section, click any of the on/off switches to allow requests (on) or deny requests (off).

# Troubleshooting

# 24

Everybody has experienced computer troubles at one time or another. It might have been something as minor as a piece of software that freezes a computer, or perhaps you've encountered a more worrisome system failure. Windows 10 has many built-in tools that you can use to solve these problems and get your computer back on track, such as System Restore to restore your computer to an earlier time when it was functioning well; Remote Assistance to allow another person to take over and fix your computer; and Task Manager, which you can use to exit an app that's become nonresponsive.

Also, you can find help for your problems with the Get Started app, which is like a high-tech user manual that provides information about a variety of Windows 10 settings and features. You can also search for help using Cortana to assist you in locating settings on your computer, or online articles and blogs about a topic that might help you learn from other users' experiences.

# Searching for help using Cortana

To a great extent, Cortana has become your new help system in Windows 10. Using Cortana, you can search for a setting on your computer or search online for help from articles and Microsoft documentation. Also, you can scan blogs where you might find the answer you need posted by a Microsoft expert or another user.

To have Cortana respond to voice commands using the "Hey Cortana" greeting, open the Cortana panel and then click the Settings button. In the Settings window, click the Let Cortana Respond to "Hey Cortana" switch to On.

## Find help using Cortana

1 Click the Cortana search box, and then type a word or phrase. Alternatively, say "Hey Cortana" or click the microphone button and then ask your question.

2 Click an item in the results to open a setting or view web content.

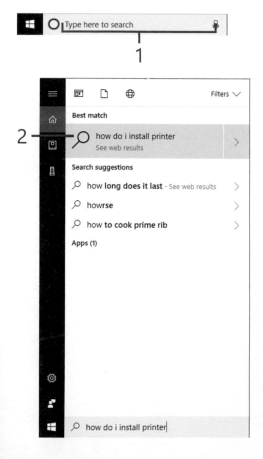

> ✓ **TIP** When you search for help using Cortana, she searches using the Bing search engine. Very often it's important that you get the most current information because technology changes so quickly (you don't want results about Windows 7 when you're trying to find information about Windows 10, for example). If you click the Web button in the Cortana search box, you can then use the drop-down list at the top of the search results in Bing, which, by default, is labeled Any Time. You can then choose a timeframe, such as Past 24 Hours, Past Month, or Past Week, to narrow your search results.

# Using Task Manager

When you are working with Windows 10, a setting or app can become nonresponsive. You might find that you're no longer able to make a choice or type text or close the window, which makes it impossible to proceed or even use any other settings or apps. When that happens, you can use Task Manager to exit the nonresponsive app and get back to work.

## Use Task Manager to exit a nonresponsive program

1 Right-click anywhere on the Windows taskbar. (Or, on your keyboard, press Ctrl+Alt+Del.)

2 Click Task Manager.

*(continued on next page)*

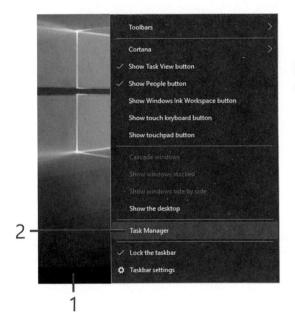

> **TIP** You can also use Task Manager to go to the Lock screen, switch users, or sign out of a user account. If your problem involves an app, by signing in as administrator you might be able to access other settings and tools to resolve your issues.

## Use Task Manager to exit a nonresponsive
## program *continued*

**3** Click a running app.

**4** Click End Task.

**5** Click the Close button.

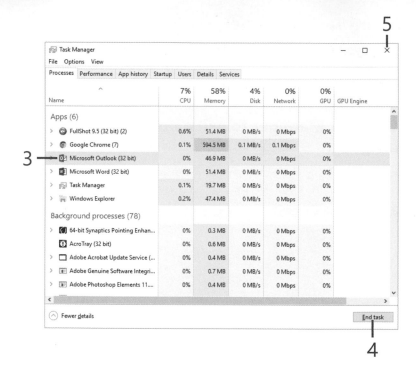

# Restoring your system to an earlier time

With Windows 10, you can create a *restore point*, which is a point in time at which you saved your computer's settings (when everything was running smoothly). If you experience problems later, perhaps after installing a new app or changing your settings, going back to a time before that change could solve problems. Before you can create a restore point, you must turn on system protection for a drive.

## Create a restore point

**1** In Cortana's search box, type the words **create a restore point**.

**2** In the results, click Create a Restore Point.

*(continued on next page)*

---

**TIP** To turn on system protection for a computer drive, in the System Properties dialog box, on the System Protection tab, click the Configure button. In the Restore Settings section that opens, select the Turn On System Protection option, and then click OK.

## Create a restore point  *continued*

**3** Click Create.

**4** In the text box, type a name or description for the restore point.

**5** Click Create, and then, when the process is complete, click the Close button in the confirmation that appears (not shown).

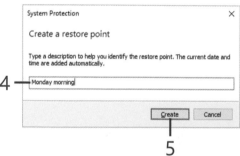

> **TRY THIS**  After creating a restore point, if you experience problems, go to the System Properties dialog box shown in step 4, and then click the System Restore button. Follow the instructions, selecting the restore point you want to use and confirming the system restore.

# Getting help from the Tips app

When you encounter a problem or can't figure out how to accomplish something, you can turn to the Tips app. This built-in app is like a constantly updated user manual for Windows 10. A series of articles with images and links to additional information are categorized into topics such as "Get Connected" and "Cortana: Your Personal Assistant." You can also go to the "What's New in Windows 10" section to see an overview of new features in the Windows 10 Fall Creators Update.

## Use the Tips app

1 Click within the Cortana Search box in the taskbar and enter **Tips**.

2 Click Tips in the search results.

*(continued on next page)*

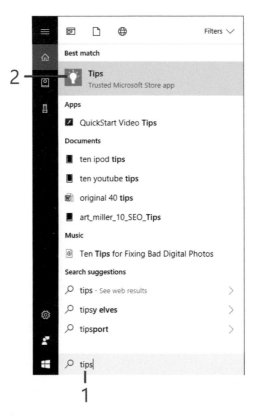

## Use the Tips app *continued*

3 Click a general category of interest, such as Personalize Your PC.

4 Click the left and right arrows to move through the available tips.

5 Click the suggested link or button (if available) to apply the tip.

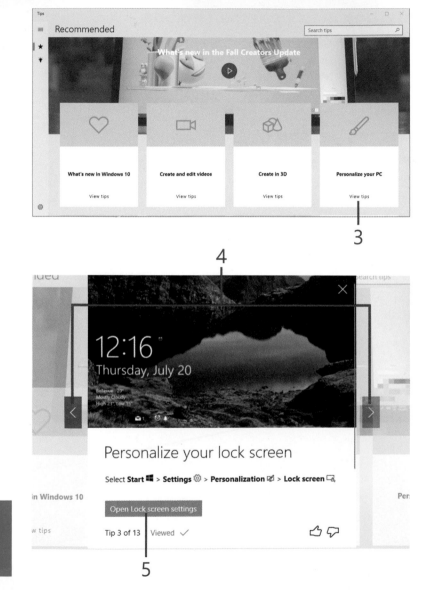

**TIP** The Tips app includes some topics other than Windows 10 settings. To learn more about the new Microsoft Edge browser, visit that section of the app. There are also sections on the Xbox app and Microsoft Office.

# Getting remote assistance

Sometimes, all you need when you encounter a problem is a little help. Perhaps you have a more computer-savvy friend or workplace associate who has offered to lend a hand, and, conveniently, she doesn't even need to be standing next to you to render assistance. Instead, you can assign her access to your computer from a remote location and let her view your computer screen, helping you to make changes to settings that might solve your problem. Note that you must turn off Windows Firewall to allow remote access to your computer.

## Get help from another user

1 In the Cortana Search box, type **invite someone**.

2 In the results, click Invite Someone to Connect to Your PC and Help You, or Offer to Help Someone.

3 Click Invite Someone You Trust to Help You.

*(continued on next page)*

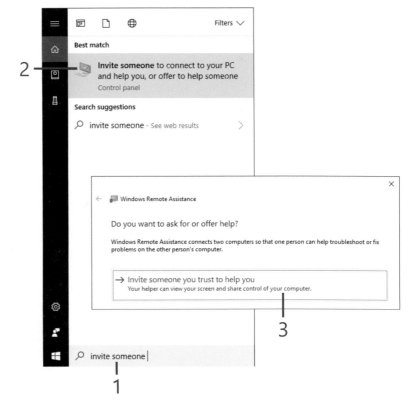

## Get help from another user *continued*

**4** Click Use Email to Send an Invitation.

**5** Remote Assistance opens your default email program and creates a new message to the person you want to help you. Enter the person's email address into the To field and then click Send to send the message.

*(continued on next page)*

4 ——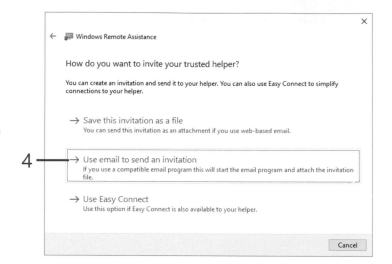

5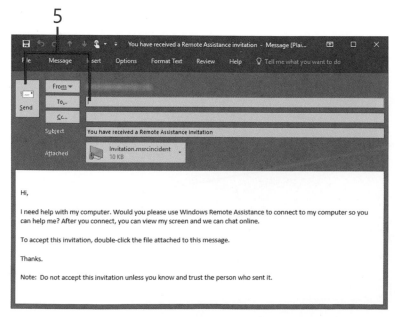

## Get help from another user  *continued*

**6** You now see a Windows Remote Assistance window on your desktop. Copy the password from this window and email your desired helper.

**7** When that person opens the email attachment and types the password, a message will appear on your screen asking if you'd like to allow access. Click Yes.

**8** To chat with the person assisting you, click the Chat button.

**9** When you and your helper have finished your session, click Stop Sharing.

> ⚠ **CAUTION**  Be sure that you know and trust the person to whom you give access. Anybody who you let use your computer via remote access can go anywhere and view anything on your computer, including personally sensitive information. Also, remember to turn on Windows Firewall again after you complete your session.

Windows Remote Assistance — □ ×
Chat  Settings  Troubleshoot  Help
Give your helper the invitation file and password
S6GZXZN9V6HT
⬇ Waiting for incoming connection...

Windows Remote Assistance ×
Would you like to allow Michael Miller to connect to your computer?
After connecting, Michael Miller will be able to see whatever is on your desktop.
Yes   No
What are the privacy and security concerns?

Windows Remote Assistance - Being helped by Michael Miller — □ ×
● Stop sharing  ⏸ Pause  Chat  Settings  Help
**A Remote Assistance invitation has been opened.
**A Remote Assistance connection has been established.
**Michael Miller has requested to share control of the computer.
**Michael Miller has been granted permission to share control of the computer.
**Michael Miller is sharing control of the computer.
Michael Miller: I think I found the problem!

Send
● Your helper is sharing control of your computer

# Using Advanced Startup

If you're having a serious computer problem, sometimes rebooting your computer—that is, turning it off and then on again—can resolve it. However, if the system files your computer uses to restart are damaged, you might need to use another method to start up. One option is to use backup system files that you stored on a USB stick or DVD. To do that, you need to use the Advanced Startup feature to restart your computer.

## Choose to startup from external storage

1  With the external storage that contains the system files connected to your computer, from the Settings window choose Update & Security.

2  In the left panel, click Recovery.

3  In the Advanced Startup section, click Restart Now.

4  On the screen that appears, click Use a Device, and then choose a device from the list that appears (not shown). Windows will now restart from your chosen device.

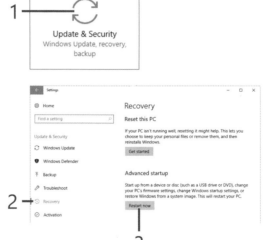

---

⊘ **TIP**  By selecting the Troubleshoot option instead of Use a Device, you can access advanced options for troubleshooting your computer problems.

# Appendix

# Taking advantage of Windows 10 keyboard shortcuts

People tend to interact with their computers in different ways. Some like using a touchscreen. Others live by their mouse. And still others prefer to turn to their keyboard to get most things done. Keyboard shortcuts provide a handy way to accomplish a great many actions by using keystroke combinations such as Ctrl+X to cut selected text from a document or Ctrl+Shift+Esc to call up the Task Manager.

In Windows 10, there are shortcuts that you might be familiar with and some new shortcuts for accessing new features such as Action Center, Task View, and Settings. Here's a rundown of some of the most useful keyboard shortcuts for Windows 10.

| Getting around Windows 10 | |
|---|---|
| Windows logo key+I | Open Settings |
| Windows logo key+D | Add a desktop |
| Windows logo key+Ctrl+F4 | Close current desktop |
| Windows logo key+Tab | Open Task View |
| Windows logo key | Open or close the Start menu |
| Windows logo key+L | Go to the Lock screen |
| Windows logo key+Q | Open Cortana |
| Windows logo key+A | Open Action Center |
| Windows logo key+E | Open File Explorer |
| Windows logo key+X | Display the desktop menu |
| Windows logo key+D | Go to the desktop |
| F1 | Open Help |
| Alt+Tab | Switch among open programs |
| Windows logo key+H | Open Share panel |
| Windows logo key+K | Start dictation |

| | |
|---|---|
| Ctrl+C | Copy |
| Ctrl+X | Cut |
| Ctrl+V | Paste |
| Ctrl+B | Bold |
| Ctrl+U | Underline |
| Ctrl+I | Italic |
| Ctrl+Z | Undo last edit or entry |
| Ctrl+A | Select active window items |
| Shift+Left | Selects one space to the left |
| Shift+Right | Selects one space to the right |
| Shift+Up arrow | Selects the previous line |
| Shift+Down arrow | Selects the next line |

## Accessibility shortcuts

| | |
|---|---|
| Windows logo key+U | Open Ease of Access Center |
| Windows logo key+Ctrl+C | Apply color filter |
| Windows logo key+Ctrl+N | Open Narrator settings |
| Shift (five times) | Turn StickyKeys on or off |
| Left Alt+Left Shift+Num Lock | Toggle MouseKeys on or off |
| Left Alt+Left Shift+Print Screen | Turn high contrast on or off |

| Working with dialog boxes and windows | |
| --- | --- |
| Windows logo key+M | Minimize all open windows |
| Tab | Move to next item in a dialog box |
| Shift+Tab | Move to the previous item in a dialog box |
| Esc | Cancel an action |
| Ctrl+Shift+Esc | Open Task Manager |
| Windows logo key+Left arrow | Snap current window to the left side of the screen |
| Windows logo key+Right arrow | Snap current window to the right side of the screen |
| Windows logo key+Up arrow | Snap current window to the top of the screen |
| Windows logo key+Down arrow | Snap current window to the bottom of the screen |
| Alt+Enter | Display properties for an object selected in File Explorer |

# Glossary

## A

**Action Center**   A panel that you display by clicking the Action Center button on the taskbar. The Action Center includes Notifications and quick settings buttons.

**Active window**   The currently selected window.

**Administrator**   A user account with administrative privileges such as the ability to modify security and other user settings.

**All Apps**   A selection in the Start menu that displays all the apps installed on your computer in an alphabetical list.

**App**   An application that provides the ability to perform a certain function such as currency conversion or playing media.

**Application**   An application that provides more complex functionality than an app, such as a word processor or spreadsheet.

## B

**BCC**   Blind carbon copy. A way to send a copy of an email to a recipient without other recipients knowing.

**Box**   Also referred to as a text box; this is a field in a form or dialog box in which you type text.

**Browse**   To use a web browser app to look for content online. Also, to browse for a drive or folder on a computer, as in File Explorer.

## C

**CC**   Carbon copy. A way to send a copy to an additional recipient or recipients when creating, forwarding, or responding to an email.

**Click**   To place your mouse cursor on a selected object and click the left mouse button to perform an action.

**Cloud**   Refers to a storage shared pool of content, apps, and documents that can be accessed from any computer, rather than being stored locally on a computer or private network.

**Command**   An option on a menu, such as Open or Save.

**Compress**   To shrink the contents of a file by encoding it with an algorithm in order to store or share that file through media with limited storage capability, such as an email attachment.

**Control Panel**   An interface for accessing certain advanced settings, used more often before the Fall Creators Update.

**Cookie**   A small file installed on a user's computer by a website to track that user's online activities. Cookies can be used by legitimate businesses to better serve return customers, but they also can be used for less legitimate purposes.

**Cortana**   A personal assistant feature in Windows 10 with which you can search your computer or the web, and instruct your computer to take actions such as opening an app or creating a reminder by voice or typing.

**Cursor**   A blinking line on a computer screen that indicates the active location within the text in a document.

**Cut**   The act of cutting an object or text from a document which removes it from that document and places it on the Windows Clipboard; you can then paste it into another location if you wish.

## D

**Defragment**   A procedure that takes pieces of files that have become separated and stored in various locations on a hard disk and arranges them in contiguous blocks. This makes it faster for a computer to find and access that content.

**Desktop**   The main interface in Windows 10 that displays active apps, shortcuts to apps and content, and a taskbar for accessing apps and various settings. In Windows 10 you can create multiple desktops that include their own active apps.

**Details pane**   A pane in File Explorer that displays details about a selected file or folder.

**Dialog box**   A window that's displayed when accessing certain settings. Dialog boxes typically contain text boxes, drop-down lists, various selections and options, and more. You use them to control an app or Windows.

**Disk Cleanup**   A procedure that deletes unused content from a hard disk to optimize performance.

**Drag**   A procedure in which you click and hold down the left mouse button on a selected object and then move the object to another location in an app or Windows.

**Driver**   A program that controls settings for hardware devices such as a printer.

## E

**Ethernet**   A group of networking technologies used to connect local area networks (LANs).

**Executable file**   A file that causes a computer to execute certain instructions, such as installing software on your computer. Though they have many legitimate uses, executable files can be used to spread computer viruses or download unwanted files.

## F

**Favorite**   In Cortana, a list of favorite places used to respond to questions or searches; also, in Microsoft Edge, a list of favorite online sites.

**File**   A storage location for computer data related to a single document.

**File Explorer**   An app used to locate and manage files and folders on a Windows computer.

**Flash drive**   A storage device for computer data that is attached via a USB drive.

**Folder**   A location for a set of stored files.

## G

**Gesture**   Movement of a finger on a touchscreen to perform an action such as scrolling or snapping windows into place.

**Gigabyte**   A unit of measurement for computer data representing a billion bytes.

# H

**Hardware**   Equipment related to computing such as a central processing unit (CPU), monitor, printer, and so on.

**History**   In Microsoft Edge, a listing of recently visited sites.

**HomeGroup**   The name for a group of computers that have been set up to access the same home network.

**Home page**   The first webpage or pages that appear when you open a browser.

**Hub**   The location in Microsoft Edge where you can view and edit Favorites, Reading List, History, and Downloads.

**Hyperlink**   Code on a webpage that, when clicked or tapped, instructs the browser to go from one location on the web to another. Also used in documents to open a web location.

# I

**Icon**   A graphical representation of an item in a software program interface, such as a button.

**InPrivate browsing**   A security feature in Microsoft Edge that you can use to browse online while blocking the downloading of cookies, temporary files, or history to your computer.

**Input**   A method of providing data and instructions to a computer such as a mouse, keyboard, or touchscreen gesture.

**Instant messaging**   A method of sending a real-time text message, image, or sound file to another person via a phone or messaging app on a computer.

**Interface**   The graphical representation of apps and applications on a computer screen.

**Internet**   A collection of computer networks that use the Internet Protocol (IP) suite to connect billions of devices around the world. The Internet supports document storage and sharing as well as access to services via the World Wide Web.

**Internet service provider**   An entity that makes an Internet connection available to computer users.

# K

**Keyboard**   An input device that can be physical or displayed on a device's screen.

**Kilobyte**   A unit of measurement for computer data representing one thousand bytes.

# L

**Laptop**   A form of computer that is portable and contains the central processing unit, a keyboard, mouse device, and monitor in one.

**Link**   See *hyperlink*.

**Live tile**   A tile located in the Windows Start menu that displays active content such as news headlines when the computer is online; a *tile* is used to open an app.

**Lock**   A state that a computer enters that stops the user from accessing the desktop unless the user provides the appropriate password or PIN for a user account to unlock it.

**Lock screen**   The screen that appears when a computer has been locked.

# M

**Magnifier**   An accessibility feature that magnifies elements on the screen so that those who have poor vision can more clearly see them.

**Malware**  A category of software that can damage data or system files of a computer or allow somebody to spy on your computing activities.

**Memory**  Also called primary storage, the hardware used to store data to be accessed immediately.

**Menu**  A feature of an operating system or software that offers commands that can be used to take actions such as saving or opening a file.

**Microsoft account**  An email account used to sign in to Windows to make email and other settings available to the operating system.

**Microsoft Edge**  A web browser built into Windows 10.

**Modem**  A piece of hardware used to modulate and demodulate (hence, the term "modem") digital data transmissions to enable communications between a computer and the Internet.

## N

**Narrator**  An accessibility feature of Windows 10 that provides audible descriptions of selections on the screen to help those who have poor vision.

**Navigation pane**  A pane on the left side of various panels and windows in apps and Windows that offers selections for taking actions.

**Network**  A telecommunications setup that allows computers to communicate with one another and share data. Network data communications can occur through cables or wirelessly.

**Notification**  An indication of an action or reminder that appears in the Action Center of Windows. Notifications can be in regard to received emails, news stories, appointment reminders, security and maintenance alerts, and so on.

## O

**OneDrive**  A Microsoft service for online storage and sharing of files.

**Online**  Having a connection to the Internet.

**On-Screen Keyboard**  A virtual keyboard that is displayed on your computer screen when you have activated a text box. You can use an On-Screen Keyboard by clicking keys with a mouse or by tapping on a touchscreen.

**Operating system**  Software that manages hardware and software functions and provides system files that enable services that support computer programs. Windows 10 is an operating system.

## P

**Password**  A user-defined collection of characters that can include text, numbers, or punctuation to authenticate that user.

**Paste**  A command used to place a copy of a file or object in another location when you have cut or copied that item to the Windows clipboard.

**Peripheral**  A hardware device that is separate from your computer but interacts with it, such as a printer.

**Picture password**  The feature of Windows by which you can unlock your computer using a picture that you choose along with a series of gestures that you make on a touchscreen.

**PIN**  A numerical code you can use in place of a password to open a locked Windows computer. The acronym stands for Personal Identification Number.

**Pin**  The action of attaching a shortcut to a program, website, or file to the Windows taskbar or Start menu.

**Playlist**  A feature of certain music player apps that you can use to add tracks from several albums to create a customized album.

**Plug-and-play**   Technology through which Windows recognizes peripherals that you attach to your computer and locates appropriate drivers to make them operable with little or no intervention on the part of the user.

**Pointer**   The on-screen icon that represents the position of your mouse on a screen or in a document.

**Power plan**   Customizable plans for how your computer handles power-draining settings such as screen brightness.

**Preview pane**   The view in File Explorer that displays a preview of a document.

**Productivity app**   A feature-rich application such as Microsoft Word or Excel in the Microsoft Office suite designed for users who make use of them in work-related activities.

## R

**Reading list**   A feature of the Microsoft Edge browser with which you can store online articles offline to read with or without a connection to the Internet.

**Recycle Bin**   A folder in Windows that temporarily stores deleted files and folders before you delete them permanently.

**Reset your PC**   A System tool that you can use to return your computer and Windows to an earlier version or reinstall Windows, keeping or removing your files in the process based on your selections.

**Resolution**   The number of pixels displayed horizontally and vertically, which can be adjusted by a user in Display settings.

**Restore point**   A point in time when you or Windows saved your system configuration. Using System Restore, you can revert your computer to those settings, possibly overcoming problems caused by later settings.

**Ribbon**   In some applications, a graphical toolbar offering groups of tools on tabs.

**Router**   A piece of networking equipment that passes data between computers on a network and the Internet.

## S

**Screen resolution**   See *resolution*.

**Screen tip**   A label that appears identifying some on-screen elements when you hover your mouse pointer over them.

**Scrollbar**   A bar that appears on the right side of some screens with which a computer user can scroll up or down a screen or webpage by dragging a box (called a thumb) up or down, clicking above or below the box, or clicking arrows at the top and bottom of the scrollbar.

**Search box**   A field in which you can type a word or phrase and then perform a search for matching data.

**Search engine**   A program that you can use to search the Internet for information by using keywords or phrases. Bing and Google are examples of search engines.

**Settings**   In Windows, a group of controls with which you manage certain features such as hardware, software, and security.

**Share**   Pertaining to the ability to share content with others via email, social services such as Twitter, print, and other methods.

**Shortcut**   A graphical icon on a Windows desktop used to open an app, setting, or file/folder with a single click.

**Snap**   A method of quickly arranging open windows side by side on your screen.

**Software**   A set of instructions to your computer to direct it to perform certain actions.

**Software as a Service (SaaS)**    (pronounced, "sass") A method of licensing or delivering software functionality from a host location on the Internet. As Windows moves toward automatic updating of its features, it is becoming a SaaS.

**Speech Recognition**    An accessibility app that makes it possible for you to speak input to your computer rather than typing it.

**Spyware**    A type of malware that involves the downloading of code to your computer with which somebody else can observe your computing activities.

**Start button**    The button on the Windows taskbar that you click to open the Start menu.

**Start menu**    A menu in Windows 10 in which you can open installed apps on your computer, open File Explorer, Settings, or Power controls.

**Subfolder**    In File Explorer, a folder contained within another folder.

**Swipe**    To move a finger or fingers across a touchscreen computer to perform an action.

**Sync**    The action of synchronizing files or settings among computing devices or between a computer and a service in the cloud, such as OneDrive.

**System Restore**    A feature of Windows that makes it possible for you to revert your computer to an earlier configuration to potentially avoid problems caused by subsequent changes in settings.

# T

**Tab**    1) A preset horizontal spacing in a word processed document. 2) A feature of browsers that you can use to access any open webpages quickly.

**Tap**    On a touchscreen computer, you interact with on-screen elements by tapping the screen. This is the same as a mouse click.

**Taskbar**    A set of tools, minimized active programs, and menus typically located along the bottom of the Windows desktop.

**Task Manager**    A feature of Windows that you can use to view the status of any running processes and stop them if necessary.

**Task View**    A view of all active programs that makes it possible for you to move among them easily. You also can use Task View to create multiple desktops.

**Theme**    Predesigned sets of display features such as color, background, and font, that you can apply to your Windows desktop.

**This PC**    A folder in File Explorer that contains files located on your computer or attached storage devices.

**Tile**    A graphical representation of an app located on the Start menu. See also *Live tile*.

**Title bar**    The strip along the top of an app containing the app name and tools such as those used to minimize, maximize, and close the app.

**Toolbar**    A feature of apps that contains clickable buttons for implementing commonly used functions.

# U

**USB**    A storage device attached to a computer via a USB port, or a port on your computer to which you can connect USB devices such as a mouse or keyboard.

**User account**    A unique account used to sign in to Windows on a computer. Each user account can have different settings and stored documents not accessible by other users.

**User interface**   Also referred to as UI or graphical user interface (GUI), this refers to the visual design presented to the user of software.

## V

**Virus**   A type of malware that, when opened, replicates itself causing damage to computer hard disks and data.

## W

**Web**   The documents stored on the Internet in the form of web-pages. Also known as the World Wide Web.

**Web browser**   A type of software used for navigating documents on the web.

**Web Note**   The ability to mark-up webpages with editing tools and share that annotated content with others.

**Wi-Fi**   A wireless networking technology used for sharing data among devices in the network.

**Window**   A rectangular element framed by a border and containing the interface of an app or application.

**Windows accessories**   A set of programs built into Windows such as Paint, Snipping Tool, and WordPad to provide commonly used functionality to users.

**Windows Defender**   A security program that is part of Windows that provides malware protection.

**Windows Firewall**   When active, this program blocks access to your computer from untrusted sources over an Internet connection.

**Windows Update**   A feature of Windows with which you can manually or automatically download and install updates to the Windows operating system.

# Index

sharing documents via email, 70
Start menu, 62
tools and menu commands, 64
programs. *See* apps
properties, displaying, 286
public networks, 107

## Q

questions, posing to Cortana, 37

## R

Reading List, using in Edge, 122
Reading view, opening in Edge, 121
rebooting nonresponsive programs,
    273–274
receiving text messages, 136
recently visited sites, seeing, 117
recipients, replying to, 144
recording videos, 166
Recovery feature, using, 262–263
Recycle Bin, restoring items, 88
reminders, adding to calendar, 191
remote assistance, getting, 279–281
renaming files and folders, 80
renting videos, 167–168
replying to email, 144
Reset This PC feature, 262–263
resizing tiles, 60
resolution. *See* screen resolution

Restart option, 20, 33
restore points, creating, 275
restoring items from Recycle Bin, 88
ribbon, 64
rotating photos, 179

## S

saving files, 68
scanners, adding, 234–235
scheduling. *See* Calendar app
screen brightness, adjusting, 93
screen color, inverting, 90
screen contents, enlarging, 90
screen resolution, choosing, 53
Screen Timeout Settings, 51.
    *See also* Sleep option
Search feature, 74
searching
    with Bing, 272
    for content on OneDrive, 250
    content on webpages, 124
    with Cortana, 85
    for favorite places, 86–87
    for information, 36
secured networks, 106
security. *See* Windows Defender
selection shortcuts, 285
selfie photos, taking, 166. *See also* photos
sender, replying to, 144

sending text messages, 137
set up, 10
settings. *See also* Action Center; taskbar
    accessing, 284
    determining status of, 96
    expanding and selecting, 19
    locating, 6–7
    modifying, 10
    opening and closing, 23
Share panel, opening, 284
sharing
    contacts, 132–133
    documents via email, 70
    files via email, 83–84
    folders via OneDrive, 251
    photos via email, 185
    and recording games, 232
    webpages, 137
Sharing settings, configuring, 110
Shift key. *See* keyboard shortcuts
shutting down, 20, 33
signing in, 11–12
sites, browsing in Edge, 116
size of items, changing, 52
Skype
    making calls on, 16
    sharing files, 83
Sleep option, 20. *See also* Screen
    Timeout Settings

## X

Xbox app. *See also* games
    adding friends, 226
    avatars, 227
    downloading games, 224–225
    gamerpics, 227

## Y

yearly calendar, displaying, 189

## Z

zip folder, compressing files into, 82
zooming in and out
    Edge, 125
    in Magnifier, 90
    Maps app, 216